THE PENGUIN MODERN PAINTERS
A HISTORY

CAROL PEAKER

THE PENGUIN COLLECTORS' SOCIETY

First published August 2001
In an edition of 750 copies

Designed by Fred Price
Printed by Octoprint, Chippenham

ISBN 09527401 4 1

CONTENTS

Acknowledgements

I wish to thank Steve Hare, the general editor of the Penguin Collectors' Society for suggesting this book to me and for much other help, Russell Edwards and Tanya Schmoller, John Curtis, Valerie Holman and Lillian Browse for answering queries about Penguin Books or wartime publishing in general. I was extremely grateful to Hannah Lowry at the Penguin Archive in Bristol for her patience and kind words, and to her colleague Michael Richardson, who likewise provided useful information. Special thanks, too, are due to Fred and Val Price for designing this book. Mike Lipkin, Ellen Swift, James Duckworth, Catherine Draycott and James Orton kindly read the text and offered valuable editorial suggestions, and Sanjiv Patel provided endless encouragement. Most of all, I would like to thank my parents for their support.

Excerpts from unpublished letters are published with permission from the Penguin Archive in Bristol and the Imperial War Museum in London.

Quotations from books listed in the Bibliography are acknowledged in the text, and covered by their 'fair use'convention, which permits short quotations without specific consent from the authors, to whom I owe my thanks.

C.P.

INTRODUCTION

STUDYING the early development of Penguin Books, once the fog of mythology and speculation thins, certain patterns begin to emerge. The Second World War was the turning point; when the example set by the phenomenally successful *Penguin Specials*, even more than the Pelicans, led the way towards Allen Lane's objective of Penguin emerging from the chaos not just a successful publisher, but the common man's library and university. Lane developed a unique vision that Penguin would ultimately provide affordable and definitive texts on every subject, written with authority, clarity and passion.

There were three sides to many of the most successful of several discrete ventures that added to the canon. Central to it all was the genius of Lane, in spotting an opportunity and cajoling someone uniquely suitable for the task into fronting and overseeing the series – quite often someone who had simply submitted a book idea, or even one who harboured no such ambitions at all. Those external editors then channelled their own energy and dedication into securing the very best authors, illustrators, advisors and assistants. The final piece in the pattern was the administrative excellence, dedication and attention to detail of the house editors, at that time A.S.B. Glover and Eunice Frost.

It was this combination that time after time produced whole series that matched the times and their audiences' needs and expectations perfectly – and all without the benefit of marketing theory, focus groups or anything that could be properly called 'research': John Lehmann's *Penguin New Writing*; Pevner's *Buildings of England* and *History of Art*; Carrington's *Puffin Picture Books*; Rieu's *Classics*. In many cases the waning of enthusiasm of one of the parties, or their impending retirement led to the sudden – or lingering – demise of the whole series. It took time to perfect the art of succession, and use this moment to inject new impetus into a series that was, perhaps, beginning to tire: as Kaye Webb did with Eleanor Graham's *Puffin Story Books*, and Betty Radice and Robert Baldick with the *Penguin Classics*. These series, and the *Buildings of England*, continue to thrive today.

The Penguin Modern Painters was a series doomed to peter out as Sir Kenneth Clark grew ever more reluctant even to add his name to it, and as other projects took up his time and energy. Eunice Frost, meanwhile, just wore out under the unrelenting pressure. Lane, too, rightly sensed that the audience had changed and the original impetus – the vacuum that had existed before the start of the series – was no longer an issue.

But while this book charts a gradual decline of enthusiasm – understandable from the very start given the state of the nation, the printing industry, paper supplies, the difficulty of the subject itself, the authors and artists represented – it is ultimately a celebration of triumph over the greatest imaginable difficulties.

Somehow, with depleted staff and resources, government interference, while their main output comprised thin, fragile books printed on paper so crudely recycled that whole words from previous printings are often visible, Penguin contrived to find paper of the highest quality, to engage printers equal to the demands of the most fastidious artists, and to produce a series that changed the way a whole generation thought about modern art and artists.

They performed, yet again, that most difficult conjuring trick – even a small act of magic – to popularise an area of culture without ever debasing it; to make it universally accessible without trivialising the subject or insulting the intelligence of their audience. *The Penguin Modern Painters* remains an object lesson for so much of today's popular press, television and, ultimately, the internet.

Steve Hare

BACKGROUND

IT would be easy for someone who knew little about the publishing history of the twentieth century to overlook the significance of a *Penguin Modern Painters* volume. They might flip through the large landscape-format Henry Moore paperback, touched as it is by wartime austerity, and dismiss it as an unimportant relic, dated, a bit dull in terms of reproductions by today's standards, a cheap charity shop throw-away. Today, after all, even the broadsheets come resplendent in colour with a good quality of reproduction. But as book collectors would know, when the founder of Penguin Books, Allen Lane, approached Sir Kenneth Clark, then Director of the National Gallery, with the idea of producing a series of modest little monographs on modern painters – particularly on British painters – he was actually positioning himself at the front of a small revolution in British art book publishing. As with many of Lane's publishing ventures, the twenty-odd volumes produced between 1944 and 1959 mostly under Clark's aegis, were unlike anything England had seen before.

If you were to browse the displays of an English bookshop in 1940 you might come across volumes such as R.H. Wilenski's *Modern French Painters,* published by Faber and Faber. Large, unwieldy, and teeming with Wilenski's scholarly ruminations, the tome was something of a Bible among the cultured set, and indeed weighed about as much as a large quarto Bible. Like the majority of art books of the time, it was an elitist and expensive proposition. Nearby you might discover Zwemmer's tall folios – co-editions which originated in Europe and were reproduced (often in limited editions) for English consumption. These marvellous volumes on subjects like *Masterpieces of French Painting* were less formidable but designed equally for a select audience, and their luminous colour reproductions and generous borders so increased their cost as to put them out of the range of the average consumer. In those days, art was highbrow and serious, obviously not the demesne of the general public, so why indeed should there be popular art books?

If accessible art books were a rarity before the publication of *The Penguin Modern Painters* series, rarer still were books on British artists. Faber preferred to produce monographs on artists like Rubens; and while occasional 'Charts' and 'Reflections' on British artists made brief appearances, not even Constable was permitted a volume of his own. Though, in the early Twenties, a small London publisher called Ernest Benn brought out a modest hard-cover edition containing black-and-white reproductions of work by British artists, by 1939 these were long out of print and long forgotten. As Lillian Browse, who as a determined young woman organised exhibitions at the National Gallery during the Blitz, recalls, 'at the outset of war there were no informative catalogues or any books to which it was possible to refer; not one single volume on a living British painter', and if there were art books around, most of these 'were written in German'. It is hard to imagine, but by Kenneth Clark's account, in the 1930s even painters as famous as Leonardo da Vinci were 'still being explored' in texts of art folios. Books about British artists were virtually an unknown quantity.

Against this backdrop, the *Penguin Modern Painters* series begins to look a lot more significant. Not only did it fill bookshops with colourful lightweight volumes at prices all could afford, it brought to England's staid armchairs work by the sort of living British artists who thought nothing of making the pilgrimage to Paris to discuss 'significant form' with Giacometti and Picasso, or taking tea in Hampstead with Naum Gabo. With his usual perspicacity, Allen Lane had decided that if the public was up to reading cheap editions of Shakespeare or André Maurois, they were up to British Modernism. Lane made his purpose clear in a letter to Clark in June 1942:

> I think you may know that for some time I have been interested in the idea of trying to do the same sort of work for the modern British artist as we have been doing for their opposite numbers, the authors, in introducing their work in a far wider field than has been attempted hitherto. The scheme I have in mind is a series of short monographs, each devoted to a particular artist and containing reproductions characteristic of his work.

Though Lane was guided by his usual impulse to edify, entertain, and make some money into the bargain, his plan, in fact, amounted to the democratisation of books about art. Faber's 1940 *Modern French Painters* was 424 pages long, printed in a first edition of 2,000 and cost thirty shillings. Penguin's monograph on Henry Moore had 16 pages of introduction, 32 plates, was printed in a first edition of 24,000, and sold for 2/6d. In Penguin's hands the art book shed its class distinctions and reached out towards a new broader audience, which greeted it zealously. Impressive sales figures in the first six months indicated what Lane already knew, that the public was not as philistine as many pre-war publishers had assumed.

★

The idea for *Penguin Modern Painters* did not just emerge out of the ether. Just as with the evolution of a species, when a great idea evolves, a lot depends on the right kind of environment. During the first four decades of the twentieth century, while the British public was still grappling with da Vinci and bristling over European Modernism, British modern artists were staging exhibitions, publishing grandiose manifestos and little magazines, and establishing a small niche for themselves alongside Europe's modern masters. The inroads British art was making into the public's consciousness may have been few and far between, but activity in artistic spheres was flourishing.

The first great stir in the British art world after the turn of the century came when the Bloomsbury art critic Roger Fry staged two Post-Impressionist exhibitions at the Grafton Galleries in 1910 and 1912. Fry had collected together paintings and sculptures by the likes of Matisse, Manet, Gauguin, Cézanne, Van Gogh, and Picasso – popular enough artists today, but back then the unwitting perpetrators of shock and scandal. Accustomed to traditional representative modes of painting, the public reacted in much the same way many people today respond to, say, Damien Hirst. As Raymond Mortimer recalls in his volume on Duncan Grant:

> Rubicund clubmen in tall hats flocked to guffaw at the masterpieces of Cézanne; in front of paintings by Van Gogh and Matisse ladies in feather boas brandished angry parasols or broke into peals of carefully silvery laughter. Eminent physicians diagnosed the types of ophthalmia or insanity from which the painters must suffer, learned critics vied with ingenuous Academicians in the virulence of their abuse.

Mortimer wasn't exaggerating. One of the doctors who would treat Virginia Woolf gave a lecture on the pictures, calling them 'the work of madmen'; and a critic in the *Morning Post* said the exhibition could be of interest only to 'students of pathology and the specialist in abnormality'.[1] Many people saw Post-Impressionism as a sign – along with socialism and the suffragette movement – of social deviancy. However, attitudes changed over time; as one commentator rightly predicted after the first Post-Impressionist exhibition: 'Cultured London is composed of clowns, who will, by the way, be thoroughly ashamed in twenty years time and pay large sums to possess these things.'[2]

The press, the public, and the so-called intelligentsia may have been alarmed by the Post-Impressionist exhibitions, but the introduction of new forms of art into England meant that English artists would never see the same way again. Artists started exploring hatching techniques and the 'primitive' quality of Picasso's pre-Cubist paintings in their own work. Roger Fry initiated his Omega workshops which investigated the Post-Impressionists' use of strong design and colour in the applied arts. Other artists, likewise inspired by the Continent, took up Futurism, Cubism and Vorticism. In 1914, Clive Bell wrote his ground-breaking work *Art*, in which he formulated his belief that aesthetic experience relies upon the recognition of 'significant form... a combination of lines, colours and forms that move one aesthetically' rather than upon representation.

During this pre-war period, many of the future series' artists were children or adolescents – though a few, like Duncan Grant, were ascending rapidly in their careers. Whatever the case, there can be little doubt that Post-

1. Hermione Lee, *Virginia Woolf* (London: Vintage, 1997), 291. The doctor was T.B. Hyslop. *The Morning Post* critic was Robert Ross.

2. 14 December 1910. Quoted in Richard Shone, *Bloomsbury Portraits, Vanessa Bell, Duncan Grant and Their Circle* (London: Phaidon, 1993).

Impressionism irrevocably altered British art and laid the foundations for much of the experimentation we can discover in the pages of *The Penguin Modern Painters*. A new era had begun in which an artist's successful communication of 'the emotional significance which lies in things', became more important than the accurate representation of nature.

The era of grand posturing and radical experimentation came to an abrupt stop with the First World War. Though the war inspired some of Britain's best works of modern war art, it also left the art world shattered, both spiritually and physically. In its wake, artists like William Smith went to the country to recover from shell-shock; Edward Bawden tucked himself away in a cottage with fellow artist Eric Ravilious, to 'get back to nature'; and many artists turned their gazes inwards, to the texture of England's historical landscape – her megaliths and standing stones, and ancient inland hills. 'Now that the artist was in England again, in woods and valleys from which evil spirits had long ago absconded,' wrote Herbert Read in his volume on Paul Nash, 'the faculty could work with more joyful effect, to reveal the immemorial values in the natural scene.'

The return to British landscape, however, did not mean that the lessons of the Post-Impressionists were forgotten, or that art stood still, rather that artists were engaged in a process of synthesis and incorporation. 'Since 1918 there has been a general return to realism,' a critic for the *Edinburgh Review* wrote in 1921: 'but the experiments of the extremists are not valueless. They have widened the horizon of painting and opened the road to a new realism in which the firm structure and rigid design of the Cubists will be combined with a truth and beauty of colour derived from the expressionists. But the wisest artists of all will be those who, like Mr John Nash, follow the advice of Van Gogh and pay heed not so much to the teaching of painters as to the teaching of nature.'[3]

Of the various groups that assembled during the 1920s, some were more progressive than others. An important one was the Seven and Five Society – composed of seven artists and five sculptors – which was formed between 1919 and 1920. Collectively the group pronounced what many other artists at the time felt: 'There has been of late too much pioneering along too many lines in altogether too much of a hurry.' The object of the 'Seven and Five' is merely to express what they feel in terms that shall be intelligible, and not to demonstrate a theory nor to attack a tradition.' Even more staid, was the London Group, which was something of a remodelled Bloomsbury, and which dictated fashions during this decade. Despite the fact that Bloomsbury had served the London art world an electric shock with the Post-Impressionist exhibitions in the 1920s, they were perceived as clinging somewhat too dogmatically to the Parisian example. As one commentator rightly noted, under Roger Fry's influence 'sedulous and

3. Frank Rutter, 'Extremes of Modern Painting, 1780-1920,' *Edinburgh Review* (April 1921), 314-15.

dowdy imitations' of French art were beginning to clutter London exhibitions. By the end of the decade, British artists grew frustrated with the Bloomsbury hegemony and tired of what some art historians describe as England's period of insular Modernism. New things were afoot abroad, and many artists were determined to be a part of them.

It was thus, during the 1930s, that Britain saw her second flowering of Modernism. The 1930s were a decade of internationalism: artists trotted across the globe; European émigrés fleeing totalitarian regimes collected in North London; and political ideas mingled with, and informed, aesthetic ones. Non-figurative art became associated with a 'free' international style, and British artists, eager not to lose pace, dipped their brushes into the turbulent waters of abstraction, Constructivism and Surrealism. Groups formed and dismantled; experimentation vied with the advantages of realism; and British artists began to take their places alongside the continental avant-garde.

One group, described by art critic Herbert Read as 'a Nest of Gentle Artists' (after Turgenev) all lived within a five-minute walk of each other in Hampstead. Ben Nicholson, Barbara Hepworth, and the ruddy Yorkshireman Henry Moore comprised the core of this group, and Paul Nash, already renowned for his book illustration and his bitter pastel reflections on the carnage of the Great War, presided over them as 'the *grand seigneur*'. The Hampstead group was in fact more Modernist fortress than gentle 'nest', and by British standards at least, their methods were bizarre and wildly experimental. Barbara Hepworth, who put holes in her sculptures, eschewed any relationship with the human form, and Ben Nicholson took abstraction to new extremes with his minimalist reliefs – which often amounted to white geometric cut-outs glued onto white backgrounds. Read, who was rapidly becoming England's foremost proselytiser for modern art, joined the 'nest' when he moved into one of the studios near Ben Nicholson:

> I remember how when we had just moved into the studio and freshly decorated it, woodwork pale blue, walls white, Ben Nicholson came in to see the result. 'Wait a minute', he said, and retired, coming back a few minutes later with a round cork table-mat which he had painted scarlet. He seized a ladder and nailed the scarlet disc high up on the white wall. The whole place was transformed with this accent of colour, perfectly placed.[4]

The Hampstead Group wouldn't see eye to eye with everyone in the new British avant-garde, or even with each other. But Nicholson's action in Read's studio was in some ways symbolic of the way the group splashed colour onto the British art scene. They were radical, they overthrew some of the apathy and conservatism which had taken hold, and dragged British Modernism, sometimes painfully, from the doldrums.

4. Herbert Read, 'A Nest of Gentle Artists,' *Herbert Read, A British Vision of World Art*, eds. Benedict Read and David Thistlewood (Leeds: Leeds City Art Galleries in association with The Henry Moore Foundation and Lund Humphries, 1993), 59.

In 1933, Paul Nash joined forces with Edward Burra, Frances Hodgkins (briefly), Henry Moore and Ben Nicholson to form Unit One, a group which brazenly declared itself as 'the modern movement in English architecture, painting and sculpture'. Herbert Read became the spokesman for the group, and a difficult and outspoken Australian art critic and collector, Douglas Cooper, acted as secretary. Unit One denounced the Bloomsbury ruling élite, eschewed the 'literary' tradition of English art, and employed sensationalist tactics to garner publicity. At the group's inception, Nash – a born ringleader – wrote a provocative letter to *The Times* challenging opponents, and stating (in direct opposition to popular trends in British art at the time) that Unit One preferred matters of Design to Nature, and wished to explore the imagination, in a way 'apart from literature or metaphysics'. (Much of the letter is quoted in Herbert Read's introduction to Nash's monograph.) In 1934 Unit One's exhibition at the Mayor Gallery aroused more attention than any since Fry's Post-Impressionist shows more than twenty years earlier.

Meanwhile, Ben Nicholson was similarly using muscle and grit to impose his 'advanced' vision on the world. In 1935, he persuaded the Seven and Five Society to shrug off its moratorium on progressive art. Soon afterwards he engineered a purge of artists unwilling to eliminate all references to the visible world from their work. The group became known thereafter as the Seven and Five Abstract Group, and in October, they staged England's first show comprised entirely of British abstract art, including, among work by other exhibitors, pieces by Ben Nicholson, Henry Moore, Ivon Hitchens and John Piper.

As the 1930s proceeded, and Hitler became ever more hysterical in his denunciations of 'degenerate art', London artists were joined by a growing diaspora of refugee artists from continental Europe. In 1935, the Hungarian-born artist and art-theorist Lazlo Moholy-Nagy found lodgings in Hampstead, as did Naum Gabo, a Russian Constructivist who made geometrical models out of string. And in 1938 the Dutchman Piet Mondrian set up a studio not far from Ben Nicholson. Gabo and Moholy-Nagy reinforced the Hampstead Group's Constructivist leanings, and in 1937 they produced a manifesto called *Circle* with Ben Nicholson and Gabo as joint editors. Although some intellectuals responded to the newcomers with jealous hostility, their presence gave many British artists the opportunity to participate as equals in the international scene. Before long exhibitions were held in which British art was placed side by side with the work of these 'exotic' foreigners.

The most colourful invasion from the continent may well have been the Surrealist movement. Surrealism was based on André Breton's notion that all art should stem from the unconscious. But it also assumed political dimensions which attracted the interest of many artists during this period of political unease. In 1936, the first International Surrealist Exhibition took place in the New Burlington Galleries in London:

Eleven hundred and fifty people crowded into the Galleries to hear Breton speak. Sheila Legge, the Surrealist phantom, walked through the assemblage, her face covered in roses, dressed in a long satin dress, coral red belt and shoes, black silk stockings and long rubber gloves. She held a dummy leg in one hand and a pork chop in the other. Since the rooms were stiflingly hot, she soon had to discard the chop. Dylan Thomas offered boiled string in tea cups, enquiring, 'do you want it weak or strong?' The newspapers were intrigued by the strange events of that day, paying morbid attention to Mme Breton's green fingernails.[5]

Herbert Read's opening speech was equally intended to alarm: 'Do not judge this movement kindly. It is not just another amusing stunt. It is defiant – the desperate act of men too profoundly convinced of the rottenness of our civilisation to want to save a shred of respectability...' Caught up in the high spirit of the exhibition, many artists remembered becoming Surrealists 'almost overnight'.

While the English abstractionists were pronouncing that abstractionism had invalidated all other forms of painting, and the Surrealists were boiling up string tea, other groups, such as the Euston Road School, went to the opposite extreme and rejected non-figurative art altogether. The Euston Road School, of which Victor Pasmore was a member, sought to re-establish what Pasmore's colleague William Coldstream described as 'the broken communication between the artist and the public'. Its artists took a sober approach to painting, confining their output to landscapes, nudes, portraits and still lifes. The Euston Road School was closely aligned with Bloomsbury (which the new avant-garde viewed as anathema), Fitzroy Street, and the largely Marxist Association of International Artists (AIA), a group dedicated to exposing political and urban squalor through Socialist Realism.

In such a climate of intellectual ferment, conflict between the camps was inevitable. In 1938 the AIA, supported by heavyweights William Coldstream and Graham Bell, called for a debate with the Surrealist factions. It was really a call to arms. However, the Realists had underestimated the Surrealists' arsenal: during the debate two unexpected spectators, Picasso and Miró, showed up and glared rather uncompromisingly from the audience, reducing the Realists to ineffectual muttering.

The critic, Herbert Read, who had quietly watched the spectacle from the sidelines, would write in the *London Bulletin*: 'We have tried to remember anything contributed to the debate by Graham Bell and William Coldstream... but there is only the stammer and the sweat.'

Even those artists who took abstraction and Surrealism on board debated its merits heatedly. The Constructivists and the Surrealists for all their similarities, professed irreconcilable differences, the one denying the real world altogether, and the other using the real world

5. James King, *The Last Modern, a Life of Herbert Read*, (London: Weidenfeld and Nicolson, 1990), 161.

as a starting point. Herbert Read, who was sympathetic to both camps, often felt 'in the position of a circus rider with his feet placed astride two horses'. Other divisions tended to rise up between artists who had a religious commitment to abstraction (such as Ben Nicholson) and those who felt it was a useful tool (such as John Piper); or those who believed that there was such a thing as 'Englishness' (such as Paul Nash) and internationalists who felt English artists should empty themselves of provincialism. Disagreements between the various camps didn't stop many artists from exhibiting with the Surrealists one day and the Realists the next, and it was not uncommon for artists to embrace abstraction one moment and to reject it, at least philosophically, later. The groups flowed in and out of each other; the trends were amorphous.

In many respects, *The Penguin Modern Painters* series was a natural product of thirty years of outlandish experimentation, factional wrangling, and bold aesthetic and philosophical enquiry. By 1940, the fieldwork in English Modernism had been done. England's new avant-garde was now sophisticated and unique enough to merit the sort of attention a series of good monographs could provide. And they were joined, in sympathy and outlook, by some of England's best art writers.

For the very reason that it was born of a milieu of friends and rivals, artists and intellectuals, *The Penguin Modern Painters* series remains an essential reservoir of knowledge about this period, and one that has indeed been under-acknowledged. We can read books about English Modernism, accounts of the British art scene since the turn of the century, the biographies of the *cognoscenti* themselves. For the most part, these tend to arrange artists into groups and schools, rather than providing access to the artists' own internal visions. No source of information brings us closer to this period and these artists – as individuals – than does *The Penguin Modern Painters* series. As Eric Newton wrote in his volume on Stanley Spencer: 'What happened "to" Spencer counts little as compared with what happened "in" him... Properly read, his pictures are, in themselves, an adequate autobiography.' This is where the strength of *The Penguin Modern Painters* series lies. The introductions contain biographical material, but the emphasis is on the artists' creative development, on their relation to their art. Because the texts were written by writers familiar with the artists' visions, they take us not only into the artists' lives, but into their minds.

★

All this accounts for the content of *The Penguin Modern Painters*, but not for the tremendous reception of the series. The art world may well have been astir with ideas and controversy throughout the Thirties, but little of this filtered down to the general public. Until a year or two before the war the British public remained more backward than forward looking, and viewed anything new that did reach them with rather a hostile eye. 'For most people the art world did not exist,' remembers

Lillian Browse, 'except for a few eccentrics. Music commanded much more interest than art. It was thought that people in art sat on the floor and smoked Russian cigarettes.' Kenneth Clark's own testimony bears this out: 'In 1940 even Henry Moore, of whose genius serious lovers of art had never been in doubt, was scarcely a name to the general public. John Piper and Graham Sutherland were even less well known.'

So what turned a population generally apathetic towards contemporary art into voracious consumers of British Modernism? The story behind the sea-change in public attitudes has its beginnings in 1935, and involves two of the characters who helped bring *The Penguin Modern Painters* series to fruition, Sir Kenneth Clark and W.E. Williams.

William – later Sir William – Emrys Williams was born in 1896, the son of a carpenter, supposedly on a small farm in Wales. One of his first jobs after graduating was teaching literature at the Workers' Education Association, where he found himself facing students forced by circumstances to leave school at fourteen and eager to claw back the education they had been denied. Perhaps because he too had modest roots, Williams brought to the cause a missionary spirit and a passion for adult education. His dedication bore fruit: in 1931 he was appointed Secretary of the British Institute of Adult Education.

In the 1930s it became evident that there was occurring a significant enlargement of the aims and interests of adult education. Evening institutes started to provide courses in drama, music, poetry and fine art; and the radio was broadcasting with the aim of both educating and entertaining. In 1935, deciding that something needed to be done to redress the problem of what he called 'art-starvation', Williams founded the programme 'Art for the People'. Borrowing paintings from private collectors, he arranged exhibitions, lectures and informal discussions about art which took place across the country. In order to alleviate the problems the public often had digesting the more modern works, Williams planted 'observers' at the exhibitions. 'They are really spies and eavesdroppers in a friendly way,' he wrote in an essay on the programme:

> If they hear a blunt Yorkshireman say to his wife as he turns abruptly away from a picture: 'Well, that's not my idea of a cherry-tree' – or whatever it is – it is the observer's job to barge in, in a casual way, and start an argument… If you can coax people to be more expansive about why they like or dislike something, you can often enlarge their understanding.

Though the scale of these exhibitions was, for the time being, small, they were the beginning of a shift of art from the élitist realm into the sphere of the common man and woman.

It was in keeping with this desire to 'enlarge' understanding, that Williams became involved at an early stage with Allen Lane's plans to expand the newly formed Penguin Books with further series, particularly Pelican Books. Lane shared Williams' fervour for education, but not his intellectual breadth; so he relied on Williams as both sounding-board and advisor in the selection of titles. Pelican made history, science, and philosophy accessible, and they also included components on art. By 1938, the imprint included Fry's seminal book *Vision and Design*, and a collection of essays brought together under the title, *Art in England*. The aims of the latter could be read in the first paragraph of its introduction:

> Oddly enough, there is no easily accessible and up-to-date book on Art in this country for the general reader. There are historical accounts of art movements, studies of particular painters and sculptors, and various memoirs and studies by leading artists and art critics. These are all very well for the minority professionally interested in art, or for the trained amateur; but they do not meet the needs of that large and increasing section of the public which is becoming more and more interested in the visual arts and perhaps, at the same time, more and more puzzled about their present development.

As the passage attests, with improvements in education, Williams' 'Art for the People' programme and the attention-grabbing turbulence in the art world, the infection for art was starting to catch.

One event, however, did more to interest that 'large and increasing section of the public' than all the efforts of educators and art lovers combined. The event was the onset of the Second World War. As Sir John Rothenstein remembers in his book, *British Art Since 1900*, when war broke out the shift in attitudes towards culture was nothing short of astonishing:

> The public seemed to be quite suddenly transformed. The change was as pervasive as it was mysterious. Could it have been that the people who knew that they stood, for the time, alone between the Nazi nightmare and everything that the world held precious had experienced a curiosity about some of the good things that belonged to the kind of civilisation they were fighting for? Or could it have been that the fact that each night might have been their last caused many to reflect that it would be sad to die without having read Shakespeare, listened to Beethoven, seen a Rembrandt? Or was it that shortage or deprivation of amenities which had formerly been readily available made people value the arts more highly? Whatever the cause, the results were manifest everywhere, whether in an increased demand for the cheap editions of the classical authors, an increased desire to listen to the classical composers and to see fine painting and, in particular, new painting.

As publishing historian Ian Norrie commented: 'It is an unfortunate fact that nothing seems to concentrate people's minds so effectively on the appreciation of the arts as a total war.'

Ironically, while the public was getting fired up about culture, most places in England were witnessing a 'collapse of all ordinary sources of theatre and music'. The National Gallery's entire collection was whisked off to safe storage beneath a quarry in Wales and, soon after, the Tate and the Victoria & Albert Museum likewise became empty shells as their collections were billeted to remote country manors for protection from bombs. London was left virtually artless. Not only was there a great cultural void, there were few forms of entertainment except for 'girlie' shows, some cinema, and the radio. People had time on their hands and very little to do.

This is where Sir Kenneth Clark, the eventual editor of *The Penguin Modern Painters*, comes in. Clark is probably best known today as the creator of the seminal *Civilisation* TV series in 1969, and father of the politician, the late Alan Clark. But by the beginning of the war, at the age of thirty-five, he had already graduated from his post as Keeper of the Department of Fine Art at the Ashmolean Museum in Oxford, and had established himself as the Director of the National Gallery, a senior member at the Ministry of Information, and a prolific writer of books, prefaces and articles on art. In December 1937 he was offered a KCB (Knight Commander of the Most Honourable Order of the Bath).

Unlike Williams, Clark was born into a section of society known as 'the idle rich'. In his biography, he describes his father as someone who 'used to tell me with deep emotion that for two years he worked'. Although Clark, in the words of his son's immortal put-down, didn't have to 'buy his own furniture', he could well afford to have Bloomsbury-designed curtains, dinner plates from Grant and Vanessa Bell and carpets conjured up by Marian Dorn, a well-known textile and carpet designer. When Clark and his wife lived at Portland Place, their staff included a cook with two helpers, a butler, a parlour maid, a housemaid, a lady's maid, a chauffeur and a social secretary – which meant they were well outfitted for entertaining members from the upper echelons of society. However, the most splendid aspect of their home must have been their extensive collection of art – Bonnards and Braques purchased when they could be bought for £100; Cézanne oils, a ravishing nude by Renoir and Michelangelo's drawing of the Virgin and Child which now belongs to the Tate. They also owned an extensive collection of contemporary British art.

Clark shared with Williams a dedication to spreading culture, that was in some wise inspired by his art critic friend Roger Fry, who believed passionately that art ought not to be the exclusive province of a wealthy few. As can be seen in his book *100 Details from Paintings in the National Gallery*, the TV series *Civilisation*, and his eminently accessible volume, *Animals and Men*, Clark also had a particular knack for presenting culture in an entertaining and edifying way. Like Williams, Clark was a talented lecturer. What Clark had above Williams, however, was a network of friends and acquaintances and connections that ranged from Queen Elizabeth to Vivien Leigh; from the wartime Paper Controller to the most lowly and eccentric artist – provided he or she had talent.

All this put Clark in rather a good position, when war came, to initiate the greatest patronage of the arts – including the visual arts – that Britain had ever known. On the first day of war in 1939, Clark 'went round to the Treasury to ask if I might be allowed to submit plans' for a scheme similar to the War Artists scheme in

World War One. Soon after the War Artists Advisory Committee (WAAC) was formed with Clark as Chairman. In part, Clark was concerned by the cultural void that had already been brought on by the impending war; he was also inspired by childhood memories of an enthralling exhibition of Canadian War Artists at the Royal Academy in 1916. In seeking to preserve and promote British art, Clark's first thoughts were not for the common man, but for those members of the intelligentsia, who, like him, would be in most need of 'a stimulus' during the long drab days of war, and might like the chance to peer at new paintings from time to time. He also admitted in his memoirs a certain sympathy with artists, who were both his friends and his source of cultural sustenance:

> I was not so naïve as to suppose that we should secure many masterpieces, or even a record of the war that could not be better achieved by photography. My aim, which of course I did not disclose, was simply to keep artists at work on any pretext, and, as far as possible, to prevent them from being killed.

His point was that the tradition of British art must be kept alive – and this meant keeping the British artists themselves alive. Whatever Clark's motives, the WAAC's reach went much further than the cultured spheres of society; it altered the cultural fabric of Britain.

Clark's official wartime patronage of talent boded well for artists, and consequently, for *The Penguin Modern Painters*. With the unfortunate exception of Eric Ravilious, who was shot down while returning from Iceland, all the artists employed by the committee survived the war. When Victor Pasmore overstayed his leave from the army in 1942, Clark wrote an eloquent letter in his defence:

> Pasmore's record in the Army until asked to do something which was contrary to his convictions is enough to prove that he is not a shirker and is willing to do his duty as a civilian citizen. In my view his first duty to society is to paint. I would not say that about many artists; perhaps there are only half a dozen men of military age now working in England whose painting is likely to be of such value now and in the future as to outweigh anything they might do as soldiers. In this half dozen I would include Victor Pasmore.[6]

Pasmore 'soon got permission to fresco the walls of the prison corridors, and was perfectly happy'. John Betjeman, who wrote the volume on John Piper, was another contributor to *The Penguin Modern Painters* series whom Clark helped rescue from the clutches of the army, when he convinced the personnel director at the Ministry of Information to engage Betjeman as his personal assistant. At least nine of the British artists in the series were full-time War Artists who benefited from Clark's protective patronage.

The WAAC quickly set about providing artists with employment, and by some accounts, it had accumulated 10,000 pieces of art by the end of the war. Many of these were also used to illustrate the series. The

6. Kenneth Clark letter to unknown recipient, 20 August 1942. Kenneth Clark archive, Tate Gallery Archives.

committee exhibited the work at the National Gallery in several rooms permanently set aside for such purposes. Wartime austerity made the exhibitions a hugely popular distraction. They later toured England and were viewed as an important boost to morale.

Meanwhile, Clark and Williams were actively promoting art through another organisation, the CEMA (Council for the Encouragement of Music and the Arts). The CEMA was founded in January 1940, by the Minister of Education, Lord de la Warr, who wished that something might be done to brighten up life in wartime. Kenneth Clark was Vice-Chairman of the Art panel, and Williams was appointed honorary Director of Art. As a disseminator of British art, the CEMA's role was tremendous. Borrowing pictures by official War Artists from the WAAC, the CEMA put these into wide circulation. Soon original pieces of British art were displayed in provincial galleries, and in factories engaged in war production. The CEMA also reproduced lithographs of work by living British artists for Forces' and war-workers' centres; reproductions of British art could even be seen in the carriages of passenger trains. Clark's wife Jane also got involved, and turned the efforts of artists to the more practical purpose of decorating the 'large, dismal eating houses, known as British Restaurants'. As Kenneth Clark recalled, the restaurants 'were in disused parish halls, specially constructed huts, or even abandoned churches, and their interiors were not calculated to make a bad meal any more appetising'. Jane Clark arranged for artists such as Duncan Grant and Vanessa Bell to paint a series of murals, and 'John Piper decorated a derelict church in South London'.

The work of Clark, Williams and others like them would have great significance for publishers. Although Penguin was the only publisher to capitalise on the situation with a comprehensive series on modern British artists, Faber and Faber produced folio volumes on Augustus John (1941) and Sickert (1943), and Phaidon followed suit with a series including Wilson Steer (1943), John (1944) and Spencer (1945). Not only did wartime programmes publicise these artists, and the lesser established Penguin artists, they brought what was formerly an élitist realm to a mainstream audience. The far reach of state sponsorship can be seen in statistics alone. Before the war, Williams' 'Art for the People' scheme managed to organise a modest five exhibitions a year. During a period of twelve months ending in 1943, the CEMA organised 132 exhibitions of original paintings; recorded attendance for sixty-six of these was over 238,300.

In addition to a receptive market, *The Penguin Modern Painters* series owes to the War Artists scheme a portion of its art. Included in the series are memorable paintings such as Paul Nash's *Battle of Britain* (1941); Henry Moore's unforgettable tube-shelter drawings (considered by Clark to be 'the greatest works of art inspired by the war'); and John Piper's moving records of bomb damage to Britain's architecture. It also inspired Graham Sutherland's menacing depictions of *Twisted Girders*, *Burnt-out Paper Rolls* and the lurid silence of a devastated

East End Street. In the 1943 monograph on Graham Sutherland, nine of thirty-two plates were reproductions of works owned by the War Artists Committee.

For the issue on Edward Bawden, published in 1946, a total of twenty-two works came from the WAAC, and as the introduction to the book attests, it is unlikely that Bawden would have had enough standing as a contemporary artist to merit inclusion in the series were it not for his prolific work as a War Artist in the Middle East. Eric Newton was one art critic who believed that the official wartime sponsorship of art had produced marvellous effects. In the *Manchester Guardian* on the 29th April 1944, he wrote:

> The National Gallery exhibition of war art has fostered – one could say, created – a new spirit in English art. Strange and vital things are to be found in it. British artists have been given an occasion and have risen to it. Officialdom can certainly kill inspiration, but only if the officials are determined to do so or are incapable of recognising inspiration when they see it. Today in the arts 'official' has almost lost its old meaning. The National Gallery is now as much a Government department as any Whitehall Ministry. It controls art, and yet in the space of five years it has infused into it a species of vitality.

The effect of the war on *The Penguin Modern Painters* series does not begin and end with the War Artists scheme. The limitations imposed by the war in a sense forced Penguin to turn to British artists, simply because images of work by European artists were hard to come by. Ties with Continental publishers had been cut, and the emptying of the National Gallery meant that pictures of European art were as hard to unearth as the paintings themselves. The dearth of good paper and official restrictions on publishing might also have turned Penguin's hand towards British artists. A monograph on a British artist was good propaganda and more likely to secure extra grants of paper than one focusing on a European artist.

Sadly, the war also meant the great sculptural innovations of the Thirties had to be abandoned: as we see in the case of Henry Moore, sketchbooks were more viable. Under different circumstances, the series might have been entitled 'The Penguin Modern Artists' to accommodate influential sculptors such as Barbara Hepworth.

If the war made *The Penguin Modern Painters* a success, it also made realising the series extremely hard work. Clark's work promoting and safeguarding the arts during the war was invaluable, as was his advice to Penguin regarding the series. But the real unsung hero of the series was Allen Lane's right-hand woman, Eunice Frost, whose tireless work uncovering paintings locked away in country homes, arranging top-standard reproductions and orchestrating the whole series in wartime conditions is a recurring theme.

★

Anyone familiar with the series might reasonably ask, 'why this emphasis on British art?' After all, Braque and Klee and the American artists Ben Shahn and Edward

Hopper are included; a further South American volume printed in Portuguese on the Brazilian artist Portinari occasionally surfaces at book fairs and on the internet; and reading correspondence in the Penguin archive, one finds that numerous other monographs on foreign painters were mooted and then abandoned. However, if we look at correspondence and press releases, it is clear that at its outset, *The Penguin Modern Painters* was conceived as a series about living British artists. A notice announcing the series, issued in April 1944, reads: 'For several years we have had in mind the possibility of producing a series introducing the work of modern British painters to the Penguin public, but it was not until two years ago when we discussed the matter with Sir Kenneth Clark, the Director of the National Gallery, that the idea began to take shape.'

As early as 1946, Lane initiated extensive plans to internationalise *The Penguin Modern Painters*. Clark initially welcomed the expansion of the series. 'A really good choice to introduce American art,' he wrote of the Ben Shahn volume. 'It makes Spencer look strangely insular.' While in Australia in 1948, Clark even went to great lengths arranging material for volumes on Australian artists Russell Drysdale and William Dobell. Though these volumes were never realised, the success of the 1949 Klee volume further encouraged Penguin to branch out. By 1953, however, Clark saw the inclusion of foreign artists as both problematic and inconsistent with the series' aims:

I greatly admire Braque's painting and no doubt he would make an admirable Penguin Modern Painter; in fact the best of the lot. But you will realise that if you include one living French painter you change the character of the series and you will be constantly bombarded with complaints and requests that you should include Matisse, Segouzac, Rouault, Dufy, Villon, etc. etc. ad infinitum.

Despite his protestations, Braque was introduced, and overtures for yet more books on foreign artists followed. The direction of the series was forever altered. This helped spell the end of *The Penguin Modern Painters*; proposals dragged on for a few more years, but the momentum behind the series had waned. Clark's loss of enthusiasm can be felt in a letter he wrote to Eunice Frost, in January 1954:

The old scheme seemed to me valuable because it helped people to understand painters whose work they could buy, and it thereby helped the painters. I remember that this was in Allen Lane's mind when he first proposed it. The new scheme is entirely different because the painters you propose do not require help and their reputations were long ago established and none of your readers could afford to buy their works.

In some ways, it seems right that *The Penguin Modern Painters* didn't survive the transition to international painters. It was the product of the war, and the need for patriotic celebration of British culture; it was also the product of artistic investigation that thrived before the war. With victory assured, the need to disseminate patriotism along with pictures of art subsided. The long-awaited restoration of collections to the major galleries produced instead a frantic need for information about these unearthed treasures and a resurgence in interest in non-British traditions. The post-war exhibition of Van Gogh had people 'queuing for miles' outside the National Gallery; and the 1947 exhibition at the Warburg Institute, 'Britain and the Mediterranean' demonstrated England's desire to reconnect with European culture.

No doubt Penguin turned to the international art scene to keep up with the market. However, the revolution in art book publishing *The Penguin Modern Painters* had helped generate itself contributed to the series' demise. Following Penguin's example other publishers joined the small art-book bandwagon: the Faber Gallery provided several thin paperback folios containing impressive illustrations and covering everyone from Botticelli to Chagall; the publisher A. Tiranti began a Contemporary Art Series of tiny collectable paperbacks with striking black-and-white covers; and Avalon Press started a series called 'Discussions on Art' featuring subjects from prehistoric art to modern painting.

As with the Penguin books, these series were all slim, aimed at a popular audience, and affordable. *The Penguin Modern Painters* was designed as a series on British artists and it did not adapt well to a change in subject matter; even a modification in format did not bolster its prospects. But this should not be seen as a sad thing. Strangely, it was the demise of *The Penguin Modern Painters* which served to keep Allen Lane and Kenneth Clark's original vision for a series on British modern painters beautifully intact.

BEGINNINGS

IT is one of history's strange ironies that the beginning of the Second World War, a time of apprehension and imminent destruction, was for Allen Lane's young publishing company an almost magical time – the beginning of an era of great innovation and promise. Penguin Books, which Lane founded in 1935 with his two brothers Richard and John, had only recently moved from its tiny origins in the Crypt of Holy Trinity Church on Euston Road and small offices nearby, to large, purpose-built premises in Harmondsworth, then virtually in the countryside. It was now a burgeoning publishing company set to influence book-buying for decades to come. Penguin was famous not only at home but around the world as a purveyor of cheap paperbacks – ultimately on all subjects. Not the least of its wartime achievements was the creation of illustrated series and a new children's imprint: *Puffin Picture Books*, *Puffin Story Books*, *King Penguins*, and of course *The Penguin Modern Painters*. But Penguin also published books for soldiers overseas and added considerably to its Pelican list. 'Much of our luck,' Frost wrote years later, 'came from the fact that we fitted into a time of very high idealism – and a wish to share a kind of explosive creativity which was so evident in all the writers and editors who themselves had so much to express, and who needed us as a forum.' This energy and idealism compensated for the paper shortages, food shortages and personal discomforts of war.

While Penguin's offices were in Harmondsworth, Lane's morning editorial meetings were held in Williams' commodious London office. Besides Williams, the meetings were attended by the fifty-year-old editor A.S.B. Glover, remarkable not only for his erudition on everything from Russian literature to bus timetables but also for the tattoos which covered him (he took to wearing gloves at work). Then there was Eunice Frost, Lane's general aide (later a director of the company), who would arrive bearing a great basket brimming with books and proofs. Lane himself appeared at the meetings with neither books, nor a week's reading under his belt; he was more the alchemist who took the base metals – people, writers, editors – and watched them react until they produced gold. Williams reports that he was never more gleeful than when watching the sparks fly during an editorial battle. Frost described Lane as 'an entrancing spinning wheel' and 'dynamic and magnetic', and he used his personality to spin ideas into books. But it was Lane that kept their feet on the ground; his main preoccupation being 'the fascination of trade, printing and financial logistics'. For twenty years, this unorthodox quartet was the editorial mainspring of Penguin Books.

After the meeting, the group frequently relocated to a modest little Spanish restaurant in Beak Street known as the Barcelona, 'run by a genial gastronome' called Carbonnel. As Williams remembers in his memoir of Allen Lane, 'fortified by innumerable *porrons* of sturdy wine from Carbonnel's family vineyard', their lunches often lasted till the evening.

At one of these meetings in 1942, Williams put forward an idea from Sir Kenneth Clark which resembled 'Art for the People' in book form. It was for a series of monographs on modern British artists – mainly Clark's friends and War Artists. At a later meeting, Eunice Frost recollected, 'Clark drew up a list of the artists he thought should be used. He said: "If you think this is a good idea, you can cost it and we can see how many colour plates there should be, and so on".'

Williams' proposal was, in fact, the end result of two years of negotiations for similar projects between Penguin and the WAAC, of which Clark was Chairman. Penguin's relations with the WAAC are interesting insofar as they shed light on the Ministry of Information's publishing policy, and reveal what hidden forces went into making England's first series of mainstream art books. Undoubtedly, popular European art books affected Lane's output – the *King Penguin* series was famously inspired by the German Insel-Bücherei published in Leipzig before the war – and the influx of European exiles from publishing circles in Central Europe, brought many new ideas to England. However, the policies of the Ministry of Information also contributed to a paradigm shift in British publishing, which makes the WAAC, that arm of the Ministry concerned with art, of particular interest here.

When the WAAC set up shop at the Ministry of Information in Senate House, the assembled group of art pundits, artists and former Slade Professors of Fine Art all agreed it would be a good idea to publish the work of British War Artists in books and magazines. Unsurprisingly, when they drafted plans for publications on War Artists, their proposals were sumptuous; modelled, no doubt, after the books and magazines in their own collections. Their early proposals for art publications included fine periodicals to 'appeal to the intelligentsia', and books of '*The Royal Academy Illustrated* type' which were to be assembled by first-rate typographers and issued by the best publishers.'[7] A dummy magazine brought to a meeting in February 1940, included illustrations in four-colour process, a four-colour auto-lithograph, and 'numerous reproductions of other types, some including colour'. Its intended circulation was 5,000, and it was to be sold for 2/6d. Clark advised that 'those whom it would reach would be influential people who would appreciate a finely produced publication'. And the Committee as a whole decided 'that they should press for it on grounds of prestige apart from economic grounds'.[8] As for a more general audience,

7. WAAC, minutes, 29 November 1939.
8. WAAC, minutes, 14 February 1940.

they could be reached through cheap illustrated magazines like *Picture Post*.

Those who regard books and art as the food of the soul may very well agree with Clark and his committee's point of view. Why fight a war if not to protect the culture that one holds so dear? But in what was essentially a Ministry of Propaganda and Censorship, this view held little water. Ministry officials projected fears of alienation onto the working and lower-middle classes; their greatest fear being that the lower echelons would believe that only the bosses would have anything to lose from a defeat to the Germans. Propaganda had to be aimed at a more comprehensive audience; not at making life more comfortable for those who were already privileged. The MoI therefore issued guidelines for propaganda and circulated them around the offices and committees. The principle behind these guidelines was simple and pragmatic: morale was to be sustained by 'a well-planned flow of vigorous propaganda... based on a single easily understood theme or policy'. The policy was to be expressed in the phrase 'Victory Through Effort'.[9] The memorandum further cautioned, 'morale cannot be sustained by occasional speeches or leaflets (sometimes in conflict with each other) or by any *ad hoc* treatment of particular situations'. Essentially, this meant the publication of selective forms of propaganda for selective audiences was out, including luxury art publications aimed at providing solace to the intellectual elite. A final curse on the WAAC's publishing plans was an embargo on coloured reproductions and luxury publications initiated by the Treasury at the outset of war to avoid paper shortages. The embargo was lifted in October 1940, but its repercussions lingered on long afterwards, as did the credo it had symbolised.

Penguin's first point of contact with the WAAC regarding a series of books on War Artists occurred in 1940, when a man named Wellington submitted to the committee the proposal 'that War Artists' work be brought out in Penguin Books at not more than 1/- each in large numbers for wide distribution' and that these books should 'contain lithographs specially drawn'. Robert Wellington was an entrepreneur with an interest in culture who had produced reproductions (printed in Germany) of Impressionists and Post-Impressionists and then sold them at Zwemmer's before the war. This was just a preliminary for what he really wanted to do, which was to involve living artists in the art of lithography. In those days, photo-mechanical reproductions were quite often a travesty of the artist's intention. The myriad hues of the palette were confined to the range of the four-colour process, and reproductions were generally approximations. Lithography – in which artists painted directly onto plates – was one way of producing reproductions which retained the vitality of the original. In 1936, inspired by the example of French limited-edition lithographs, Wellington, along with his friend John Piper, established a company called

9. Memorandum, *Notes on the Present Morale Situation*, 3 July 1940, PRO file: INF 1/234.

Contemporary Lithographs. Besides making reproductions for the wall, not the portfolio, their intention was to bring 'good and inexpensive art to school children' to help develop their taste and artistic sensibility. Soon twenty-five artists – including the likes of Piper, Paul Nash, Ivon Hitchens, Frances Hodgkins and Graham Sutherland – were visiting the printing works of the Baynard and Curwen Presses and making drawings on the stones or plates. The project was undermined by various factors: the onset of war which meant that many of the artists were occupied as War Artists and didn't have time to visit the press, the bombing of the Curwen Press, and Harold Curwen's mental ill-health. In an attempt to get things started again, Wellington developed a proposal with Lane for War Artists' lithographs and then submitted it to the WAAC.

At the MoI, the proposal was greeted half-heartedly. Lithographs had been growing in popularity before the war, especially in publications like *Signature*, but in wartime, the idea of original lithographs by War Artists was both impracticable and unorthodox. The WAAC decided to pursue the option of producing 'books with good reproductions of existing War Artists' work, all or some in colour...' and agreed that, at the very least, Captain Ravilious might be asked to provide some original lithographs. Wellington refused to consider anything but lithographs. And when Captain Ravilious said he wasn't willing to draw lithographs to Penguin's specifications, for the time being, talks with Penguin ceased.

A couple of months later, Sir Kenneth Clark had a meeting with the Director General of the Ministry of Information at which the publishing aspirations of the WAAC were discussed. Clark, who was in any case beginning to suspect that his background might represent a handicap to his judgment in producing propaganda, agreed to lower his sights.[10] At a meeting in December, the committee abandoned their plans for auto-lithographs and four-colour processes, and decided to aim for books containing 'satisfactory' reproductions in monochrome, with 'the widest possible circulation'. Following the decision, they invited Penguin, along with Oxford University Press, 'to submit proposals for 1/- books on separate topics, each with a large number of reproductions in monochrome'.

Lane went to great lengths to secure the contract, but in the end the more staid and conservative Oxford University Press won out. The OUP was already engaged in producing other propaganda booklets for the Ministry, most notably its Pamphlets on World Affairs of which seventy were published before 1945. But Clark obviously regretted the missed opportunity to work with Penguin, as he wrote to Lane:

> I know that this decision will be a disappointment to you, and I am sorry that owing to the slowness with which the Oxford Press made up its mind I let you go to so much trouble on our behalf. It is not for me to question the

10. Ian McLain, *The Ministry of Morale: Home Front Morale and the Ministry of Information in World War II* (London: George Allen and Unwin), 97.

decision of my Committee, but I shall always feel grateful for the enthusiasm with which you greeted the project when it was first put to you.

★

The OUP produced eight innocuous little booklets filled with mentions of heroes and the war effort and shabby monochromes – pure, unadulterated MoI propaganda. The most artful things about them were the introductions, in which their authors wrote apologetic justifications for the production of art in a time of war. Strangely, the ugly little books sold extremely well: the first four editions of 24,000 were snatched up within six months and the press clamoured for more volumes on fresh subjects. They were unattractive, but they were small and cheap, and remain collector's items to this day. And flawed as they were, they brought a lot of work to a public hitherto unfamiliar with the joys of British contemporary art.

Clark's notions about art book publishing might have needed bringing down a peg or two, but for him the Oxford series was unacceptably low-brow even in wartime. Realising that his aims would never be achieved within the MoI, he took the back route to Penguin though Williams. Evidently Clark, who had modified his vision from élitist to mainstream, had chanced upon the right formula. Lane seized the idea, and worked his charm upon Clark until the latter offered his services as the editor of the series. 'I am writing to tell you how delighted I was to hear from my secretary this afternoon of the possibility of your being able to edit the proposed Penguin Modern Artist Series', Lane wrote, 'I didn't like to suggest this myself as I know how many calls there are already on your time.'

Lane's negotiations with the WAAC didn't end with the birth of *The Penguin Modern Painters*. In an effort to rope the MoI into supporting the project – which would enable a much greater print run – he submitted a proposal for a series of cheap monographs on *individual artists* employed by the Committee to be produced in editions of 150,000.

As he was often to do during the war, Lane baited the MoI with assurances that the books would make good propaganda, and that 'war and peace subjects were to be included'. According to WAAC minutes, 'The chairman [Clark] said that a book of this description had been planned some time ago, and it was agreed that the Secretary enquire from Publications (Information) as to the likelihood of this being produced.' Just as Clark was never able to fulfil those dreams for lavish art books and journals through the MoI, Lane was never able to entice the Ministry to back his proposals so that he might publish such books in their hundred thousands. The Publications Controller flatly rejected the proposal. But the drawn-out history of negotiations and proposals between Penguin and the WAAC brought Clark and Lane together, and the combination was fruitful.

In the letter in which he offered his services to Lane, Clark expressed some fear that Lane would not take up his offer: 'This proposal may be embarrassing to you, as you may feel that my editorship would give the series too much of a parti pris; or you may feel that I could not give enough time to it and you would rather have an editor whom you could hustle.' Clark should not have worried; as the most influential man in the London art world, he would be a great asset to Lane from the point of prestige alone. Art critics such as Herbert Read were perhaps more powerful as shapers of opinion on contemporary art, but Sir Kenneth Clark had a cachet with the middle classes. As someone with a passion for both the old masters and contemporary art, he was just the man to sell Modernism to the masses.

Lane would likewise prove to be Clark's ideal publisher. He gave him the liberty to fulfil some of his ideas about art and publishing which had been hindered at the Ministry. He shared Clark's desire to produce books about art with excellent production quality and still guided by the impulse to educate; books that didn't appeal to Clark's old bugbear, the lowest common denominator. Lane had the foresight to see that quality and mass production needn't be antithetical.

As *Penguin's Progress* reported in July 1946: '*The Penguin Modern Painters* series, edited by Sir Kenneth Clark, was designed to bring the work of painters to the wide public outside the art galleries: the public who have perhaps never ventured within because they doubted their ability to appreciate what they would see.'

As a Penguin editor, Clark revelled in his unfettered freedom to promote abstract and Constructivist art, forms which were not encouraged by the Ministry since they were seen as challenging, and possibly threatening, rather than reassuring. During his time at the Ministry, Clark had at one point expressed regret that the War Artists collection contained no work by painters such as 'Matthew Smith, Frances Hodgkins, Ethel Walker, Ivon Hitchens, Ben Nicholson and Victor Pasmore'.[11] The artists were too 'advanced' or they were better off left to their own devices. With the exception of Walker, these artists mentioned by Kenneth Clark were all given monographs in the Penguin series.

11. Penelope Curtis, Introduction to catalogue *World War Two, A Display of Pictures from the Collection to Mark the 50th Anniversary of the Outbreak of War in September 1939* (Liverpool: Tate Gallery, 1989), 3.

SELECTION OF ARTISTS AND WRITERS

NO critic of British Modernism could, in fairness, accuse Clark of bias or preference in his selection of artists and writers for the series. Though many notable artists are excluded, such as Mark Gertler, C.R.W. Nevinson, James Pryde, Gilbert Spencer, Edward Wadsworth and Christopher Wood, on the whole Clark showed remarkable foresight in choosing many artists who have endured the test of time as Britain's foremost Modernists. Taken together, the monographs provide ample taste of the many different schools and styles comprising the art scene in the Twenties, Thirties and Forties. It is a selection made up of checks and balances: Edward Burra's love affair with the underworld of Latin Europe is the antidote to Paul Nash's peculiar Englishness; the austere, formal minimalism of Ben Nicholson is balanced by the restful depictions of *Harbour in Snow* or *Black Swans at Chartwell* painted by his father, William; and the lurid abstract forms of Sutherland contrast with Edward Bawden's figurative watercolours of Egyptian camel markets and Iraqi sheikhs from his time as a War Artist in the Middle East. Then there are artists in a league of their own, such as Stanley Spencer, whose odd perspectives of his native Cookham and religious imagery speak their own uncanny language. As David Hall pointed out in a previous Society publication: 'How far Clark's personal preferences accounted for the inclusion of particular artists and the choice of authors is to some extent only a matter for speculation.'

But we can speculate. As the editor of the series, it is only natural that some of Clark's own preferences – both artistic and personal – would have come into play. It is no coincidence, for example, that of the first eleven painters in the series, nine were War Artists; that of the first eight artists featured, five counted as Clark's closest friends, and that at least twenty-three of the paintings which were eventually reproduced came from Clark's own collection. Furthermore, it is no accident that artists who dealt with figurative art, even if influenced heavily by abstraction, were more likely to be chosen than the Surrealists or the Constructivists, to whose work Clark was ideologically opposed. However, it is also likely that Clark's temptation to feature both his friends and his favourites was tempered by a concern for his reputation in an art world riven with petty rivalries. He was eager to overcome the reputation for conservatism and parti-pris politics he had amongst certain 'abstract' factions; but he also feared that the more traditional camps would accuse him of promoting his own interests by featuring the works of artists he liked, and consequently, collected. In August 1942, after gathering together some his own pictures for reproduction, these fears led him to instruct Frost: 'My name must not appear as the owner in the books, or else the Royal Academy will say that I am only editing the books to puff my own collection and then sell it.'

Still, despite such reservations, Clark did include his friends. Of the many that appear in the series Clark regarded Bloomsbury artist Duncan Grant (as well as his wife, Vanessa Bell) as his closest; it is little surprise that Grant appears among the first four published, and it was most probably the 'conspicuous similarities' between Grant's work and Bell's that prevented a volume devoted to Bell. Clark and his wife were also friendly with John and Myfanwy Piper and frequently visited their plain, square home, Fawley Bottom Farmhouse. In his autobiography, Clark fondly recalls sleeping 'in a room full of dark brown books on Gothic churches' and enjoying conversation with 'two of the most completely humanised people I have ever known.' Clark's friendship with Victor Pasmore had its auspicious beginning the day the artist wandered in on him, when he was trying a frame on a Turner painting at the National Gallery. The young Pasmore derided Clark on his choice of frame and said, 'I don't know who you are, but whoever you are you've no taste.' Clark removed the frame hurriedly and introduced himself. They remained close friends for ten years, and Clark collected over twenty of Pasmore's paintings. During the war, Henry Moore became a fixture in the Clarks' lives and Kenneth Clark spoke of him as a 'loyal and affectionate friend'. Jane Clark was fortunate to have been the recipient of one of Moore's Tube shelter sketchbooks. Likewise, Graham Sutherland and his wife lived with the Clarks in 1940 and for two years thereafter as wartime refugees. 'The Sutherlands did not recoil from smart society,' Clark wrote, 'and came frequently to our dinner parties, where they were much admired.' A less intimate friend was the elderly and rather eccentric artist William Nicholson: 'The *cher maître* had no sense of time and would sit for an hour or two in my room in the National Gallery gossiping about figures of his youth, whom he assumed that I had known.'[12]

Clark's relations with authors in the series were by no means less personal. In addition to his friendship with Myfanwy Piper who wrote on Frances Hodgkins under her maiden name, Myfanwy Evans, Clark was on good terms with Betjeman and, of course, with the Director of the Tate Gallery, John Rothenstein. After the war, Clark and Rothenstein went on an eventful trip to Paris with the intention of purchasing art. Philip Hendy was another of his associates. Clark met Hendy early in the war, when as Director of the main gallery in Leeds he organised an exhibition of the work of three of Sir Kenneth's closest artist friends: Moore, Sutherland and Piper. Hendy generously invited Clark up to Leeds to open the show. It must have been a memorable first

12. Kenneth Clark, *Another Part of the Wood: A Self-Portrait* (London: Murray, 1974), 272.

meeting, since the artists, their wives, and the Clarks all arrived in Leeds by train having downed a dozen half-bottles of Orvieto Secco along the way. Hendy, himself quite sober, met the spirited party at the railway station.[13] No doubt Clark was drawn to Hendy, who shared his passion for both the old masters and modern art and had, like him, given a great boost to the careers of the artists he admired.

It was inevitable, given his position, that Clark should have had personal contact with these people; and he came into contact with a great many more artists and writers who were not included in the series. But he was also an active patron of his friends, and as already seen, he wrote to Eunice Frost years later: 'The old scheme... helped people to understand painters whose work they could buy, and it thereby helped the painters.'

More interesting than the question of how friendship and patronage came into play, was how Clark's taste affected his judgement when it came to artists who were not his friends. At times Clark's more conservative leanings came to the fore – he was a sophisticated judge of merit, but also reluctant to embrace certain abstract tendencies. When commentating on the work of his friends, for example, he was apt to whitewash over their abstract qualities; indeed in his catalogue introduction to Graham Sutherland's first one-man show at M. Rosenberg's London galleries in 1938, he denied that Sutherland's landscapes were abstract at all: 'Nearly all the pictures in this exhibition have been painted from small, careful drawings done on the spot, squared for enlargement and followed most accurately... As a result Sutherland's work is the reverse of abstract.' Equally telling was Clark's initial response to the primitive sculptures of Henry Moore, which he unflinchingly compared to hot-water bottles (a report he later denied). Ideologically, he was positioned somewhere between the staid and old-fashioned British Academy and Read's rambunctious 'gentle nest'. He was an avid sympathiser of the Euston Road School of realists, and a close affiliate of Bloomsbury, which, as we've seen, was by this time regarded (by the younger generation of artists) as a self-serving self-protective élite. Paradoxically, it was his strain of conservatism that would make him the perfect conduit for bringing modern art to middle England.

In 1935 Clark found himself embroiled in a battle with Herbert Read in the pages of *The Listener.* In a piece called 'The Future of Painting' Kenneth Clark attacked 'advanced art' on the grounds that it was 'out of touch' with reality. 'To begin with, abstract art, in anything like a pure form, has the fatal defect of purity. Without a pinch of earth the artist soon contracts spiritual beri-beri and dies of exhaustion. The whole Cubist movement has revealed the poverty of human invention when forced to spin a web from its own guts.'

Clark wrapped up his piece with an ominous warning: 'We must keep in mind the possibility that in the

13. Roger Berthoud, *The Life of Henry Moore* (London: Faber and Faber, 1987), 177.

western world the plastic spirit is really exhausted and that art will be lost for many decades.' In the next issue, Herbert Read, England's boldest champion of 'advanced art', countered the attack, stating that reality can be defined in different ways: there are other aspects of reality of a more mathematical and crystalline nature which may equally form the basis of the artist's creations. Read's response was considered and diplomatic, but the stage was set for a bloody battle. The battle began in earnest when Clark claimed that Ben Nicholson's carved reliefs, which Read had used as an example, were too geometrical to have any real life-enhancing vitality. Soon, supporters of both sides were writing impassioned letters to the journal. In the end, artists like Sutherland and Piper privately shook their heads at their patrons' views and Clark abashedly blamed his conservative grumbling on an impacted tooth. Even as the most powerful figure in England's art world, his reputation had suffered a blow.

After such an experience, Clark was loath to engage in combative art-world politics. At the end of June 1942, when he drafted a list of the first twelve artists paired with potential writers for Eunice Frost, he added the following afterthought: 'I am a little worried at the total exclusion of Herbert Read. He himself would not object, but he is the victim of a parasitical clique of abstract and Surrealist painters who would try to make him regard his omission as a slight, and it might be wise to include him.'

Clark's desire to avoid sparring against Read's 'parasitical clique' soon resulted in another concession. In October 1942 Herbert Read wrote to Clark insisting that his old bugbear, Ben Nicholson, have a volume. Clark was bemused, and failed to take the suggestion seriously. By December, however, Nicholson had got wind of the fact that not only all his old friends – Sutherland, Nash, Piper – were to have titles, but his father was due a volume as well. The elder Nicholson belittled his son's abstract work with regularity, and after a reviewer in the *New English Weekly* described it as 'a lavatory artform', he made it a habit of goading Ben by asking him, 'done any more of them awful lavatory seats, Ben?' The inclusion of William Nicholson in the series, then, heaped salt on the wound, especially as Ben Nicholson predicted mass sales for the series. Knowing the younger Nicholson's feelings, Paul Nash took umbrage on the painter's behalf and made his inclusion in the series incumbent on that of his old Slade schoolmate.[14] Still Clark held off; he didn't like the work of Ben Nicholson, and from his publishing programme at the WAAC he was quickly realising that wartime was not the best time to thrust purely abstract work at the unsuspecting masses. In spring 1943, however, as the Allies moved on to the offensive, Clark relented. When he wrote to the architectural historian John Summerson, asking him to write on Ben Nicholson, the artist was delighted: 'I think these things pub. at 6d & 1/- are very important

14. Margot Eates, *Paul Nash: The Master of the Image*, 1889-1946 (London: John Murray, 1973), 79.

indeed as they reach the ordinary chap in a way no de luxe pub. like *Circle* can.' The commission settled, Summerson dashed down to visit Ben Nicholson in St Ives, the old Cornwall fishing port where two generations of artists had gone for inspiration from the schooners and drifters, the rugged fishermen and the dark churning sea. As Ben Nicholson's biographer Sarah Jane Checkland relates, 'the two hammered out the project together in the summer heat'.[15] The inclusion of people like Read and Ben Nicholson meant that the series did not resemble a partisan stab at representing British Modernism, but encompassed numerous points of view.

One artist who mistakenly regarded the series as the product of an exclusive coterie was Wyndham Lewis. During the heyday of the Bloomsbury artists, Wyndham Lewis had established a deep-rooted antagonism with this set, and had succeeded in backing himself into a lonely corner where he barked out defensively against most of the art world. His ire was particularly directed at Roger Fry, for 'inventing' artists such as Duncan Grant, whom he described as a 'weak and lady-like coal-heaver'. At one point Lewis had participated in Fry's Omega Workshops, but he later referred to them as an 'arty-crafty *fin-de-siècle* survival', and merrily reported that 'the chairs we sold stuck to the seats of people's trousers'. Since Lewis saw Clark as an emanation of Bloomsbury, and as Fry's logical successor, Clark inherited all of Lewis' vitriol towards the powerful art pundit and arbiter of taste. In his letters Lewis referred sarcastically to 'Bloomsbury's little tea party' and 'the great Sir Kenneth, that illustrious knight'.[16]

Sir Kenneth, for his part, respected Wyndham Lewis's painting, and it is most unlikely that personal politics had anything to do with the artist's exclusion from the series. During the war, Clark commissioned Lewis, who was stationed in Canada, to produce a painting for the War Artists Committee. Unlike the other artists who received 100 guineas for their work, Lewis was promised £300 in keeping with his other commissions, and was paid half the amount before he even started. After a couple of years, and many displays of stubbornness on Lewis's part, the committee still lacked a picture. It was not until 1947 that they first glimpsed the work, and the picture didn't really leave Lewis's hands until 1956 when he donated it to the Tate Gallery.

It may have been Lewis's propensity for tormenting bureaucrats that kept Clark from inviting him to participate in the series. In any event, Lewis took his exclusion to heart, and in 1947 he wrote to James Thrall Soby: 'In the Penguin Books of English Painters… the world is offered a very imperfect survey of British painting.' Lewis wasn't the only one who noted his absence. Several readers wrote in, suggesting him as a candidate for a monograph. As late as 1957, Penguin received a

15. Sarah Jane Checkland, *Ben Nicholson, the Vicious Circles of his Life and Art* (London: John Murray, 2000), 221.

16. Wyndham Lewis to T.J. Honeyman, 5 October 1939, *The Letters of Wyndham Lewis*, ed. W.K. Rose (London: Metheun, 1963), 266.

letter from a Sergeant D.S. Britton: 'I think your Modern Painters series is excellent. It represents nearly all that is important in modern painting, except, I think, for one appalling omission – Mr. Wyndham Lewis. I have for some time been an admirer of his fiction, and I notice that Penguin Books have failed to publish that as well.' He added as a postscript: 'Meanwhile there is absolutely no way of getting to see his magnificent drawings short of barging into the home of some private collector.'

If Clark's concerns about his own reputation came into play in the choice of artists and writers, chance and expediency also had a lot to do with the final shape of the series. An early volume on Ardizzone was to be written by V.S. Pritchett, but various hurdles prevented it from coming to fruition, and Graham Sutherland thus replaced the figurative artist as number two on the list. Likewise, a monograph on Augustus John was dropped when Clark invited Sir John Rothenstein to write on the artist and Rothenstein expressed a desire to write instead on Edward Burra. Clark was always ready to accept the opinion of those he respected; his inclusion of Matthew Smith, for example, might have been influenced by the esteem with which Roger Fry had held the artist.

As for the authors, much shuffling took place, but Clark's main objective was to match artists with authors who could write sensibly about their work. Knowing that his colleague Philip Hendy had together with Jacob Epstein curated an exhibition of Matthew Smith's work in Leeds, Clark invited the Director of the Leeds gallery to write on the artist. Initially Hendy demurred, prompting Clark to write to Frost: 'If Hendy is still reluctant, Matthew Smith has made a good suggestion, Richard Wyndham, who is himself a painter and writes well. He would in fact be better, so I will... see if I can shuffle out of Hendy gracefully.'

Thankfully, Hendy came round before Clark took this course, since the result was so good that even Ben Nicholson, who excelled at hurtling abuse at writers, enthused, 'Hendy's introduction is excellent!' An equally fortunate pairing was that of Henry Moore and his old Hampstead friend, the poet Geoffrey Grigson.

Grigson was a frequent guest at the studios of various members of the Hampstead crowd, and his magazine *New Verse* had been instrumental in introducing Surrealism into England. Of Grigson, Ben Nicholson once wrote: 'I like Geoffrey v much... – goes v deeply into the matter & is terribly good company.' In 1939, Moore provided a drawing for the jacket of Grigson's first volume of poetry, *Several Observations*. It may have been a result of Grigson's introduction to the Henry Moore volume that he was invited by the British Council to lecture on Moore's work as it toured Europe in 1949. In any event, the match proved fruitful; as the sculptor's biographer Roger Berthoud attests, Grigson's essay 'was a good deal sprightlier and more vividly perceptive than Herbert Read's pioneering study of a decade earlier'.[17]

17. Berthoud, *The Life of Henry Moore*, 189.

'I believe that Betjeman will be the best person to write on Piper,' Clark wrote to Lane. 'I could help him over the part dealing with Piper's abstract work, which he probably doesn't like. At this rate your authors are going to be almost as distinguished as your artists.' No author could have been better suited to write about the work of John Piper than Betjeman. Like Piper, whose taste for architectural lore infiltrated much of his work, Betjeman had been fascinated by architecture since childhood, and even as a young boy had cycled round villages 'noting all the varieties of early English style'.[18] In the 1930s Betjemen was well known for his Shell Guides on regional architecture, for which he recruited writers such as Paul Nash and John Piper. Piper was commissioned to do the Shell book on Oxfordshire (1938), *Oxon*, as it was entitled, and this was followed by *Shropshire*, the first collaboration between Betjeman and Piper (written in 1939, and published after the war). Richard Ingrams commented on their special relationship in his book *Piper's Places*: 'The two hit it off from the start... They had a great deal in common. They were both children of the middle class; both had rebelled against fathers who wanted them to take over the family business; both had spent their childhood and teens cycling round the countryside looking at churches.'[19] The only drawback in the alliance was Piper's unremitting energy. Betjeman used to complain to Piper: 'I can't do more than ten churches a day, old boy.' While researching the Penguin monograph, Betjemen spent his time muddling through 'the books, drawings and old canvases of [Piper's] house', and was also privy to 'confidences of which I trust these pages will not be a breach'.

Despite his openness and good sense, Clark remained to the end wary of admitting responsibility for selecting whom and whom not to include in the series. He wrote to Frost rather too casually: 'I prefer that my own name should not appear anywhere. No one ever notices who edits a series – at least I never do – and consequently no one will observe that the editor's name has been omitted.' Clark's name, of course, wasn't omitted, and his reputation only profited from association with a series remarkable for its variety and balance.

18. Richard Ingrams and John Piper, *Piper's Places: John Piper in England and Wales* (London: Chatto and Windus), 43.

19. Ibid. 44.

PUTTING THINGS TOGETHER

WHEN people write about Eunice Frost, they tend to draw one's attention to a large group portrait by Rodrigo Moynihan that still hangs in Penguin's Harmondsworth offices. The painting depicts the Penguin editors – a dozen or so men in black and two women – standing around talking casually, as if after a conference or a meeting. Never once in Penguin's history did the editors formally assemble together like this, so the scene is entirely fictional. But its symbolic role is important. At the very centre of the painting, but not in the foreground, stands a figure wearing a bright smart dress. It is, of course, Eunice Frost, the woman a colleague once described as 'the lynchpin' of the Penguin world.

Frost deserves our attention because, in many respects, the story of *The Penguin Modern Painters* series is really her story (or one of her stories); the ups and downs, the successes and failures of the series all belonged to her.

Frost joined Allen Lane's company in 1936 when she arrived at his office in Great Portland Street for an interview dressed as if for Ascot wearing a huge cartwheel hat. Lane, who was himself a rather boyish and effulgent creature, overlooked her flamboyance and installed her as his secretary on the spot. A week later he pushed a pile of books across her desk, saying: 'do you like reading?' It was an imperative addressed as a question. Frost would recall, years later, 'that's how I learned you had to carry the baby home with you every night'. Henceforth she read manuscripts, and negotiated with authors, agents, editors, printers and publishers, in addition to keeping administration on track. 'I remember,' she wrote, 'that in my very first week, instead of being told what to do, I was expected to do the extraordinary.'

Frost was barely twenty-two at the time, but she would soon prove to be the moving spirit in the Penguin world and, as a colleague who knew her later remembers, 'fearfully important in the development of the firm'. Her rise was due partly to the war, during which Allen Lane's brothers were called up for service, as were other members of the existing staff. This opened new opportunities for women like Frost to show their true potential. W.E. Williams offers up a mixed assessment of her talents: 'Women of her calibre are not rare, but in her time rarely reached a place of importance in a publisher's office. She certainly did... [Frost] revealed qualities which were to make her one of the decisive personalities of the firm.' Frost's endless tact – and energy – allowed her to orchestrate almost every series the company undertook in its early years. 'My view,' wrote Doug Rust, Penguin's Royalties Manager 1951-1993, 'is that Eunice Frost's contribution to the Penguin Fiction list outstripped any person since... she laid a foundation that the Penguin empire still stands on today.'

It is hard to know exactly who Eunice Frost was. She was ebullient, impressed people with her astonishing capacity for retaining knowledge, and was memorable for a marvellous raucous laugh. But she was also a one-way door: she gave and gave of herself in the service of others, but she never let anyone in far enough to understand what made her tick. Few people got close, though Williams seems to have regarded her with a deep paternal fondness. In January 1941 Frost collapsed – physically and emotionally – from overwork. A letter Williams wrote to her during this time is worth quoting in its entirety for its affection, its paternal advice and what it reveals about Penguin's dynamics:

My dear Frostie

As soon as you open your eyes you shall read this little scribble with no interest and enthusiasm. I know that. But, all the same, I must sit down and write it. For I am terribly sorry to hear you've been smitten down – half an hour or so, it seems, after you were bandying words with me on the phone the other day. Yet, ill as you are, I'm terribly glad that they got their hooks into you in time. I'm glad, too, that – once the pain and the dejection are over – you'll be compelled to lie in bed and rest instead of carrying Penguins on your resolute and overburdened shoulder.

A.L. is very sorry for you – yes, for you and not for himself! And your colleagues seem to have been impressing him with the fact that you've been overworking for years at Harmondsworth.

I'm utterly lost without you, my dear. I can't get anyone to do anything, and I no longer seek a pretext to ring up West Drayton. Will you take a piece of wise old gentleman's advice – as soon as things stop hurting, lean back and relax. Relax all the way thro', right to your very bones. Enjoy the vacuum of utter weariness, including the refreshment of crying into your pillow 2 or 3 times a day. Let go the mainsheet and the painter and everything else and dawdle in the twilight for a bit. I know what I'm talking about; if you take your convalescence without strain or resistance you'll come back to life on the bounce. Take it easy, Frostie my love, or I'll beat hell out of you. I'm coming to see you soon.

J.E. Morpurgo, Allen Lane's biographer, played down the importance of Frost's contribution; Penguin historian Steve Hare describes her as 'an immensely complex woman... the most acute woman I ever met'; and Saul Bellow 'loved' her because she was 'dovelike and forebearing'. 'In fact,' he wrote, 'she was angelic.' Those who worked with her found her intellect and powerful character daunting. She was a perfectionist who used to make a round of the office late at night, leaving notes on typewriters whose covers had been left off. This while juggling in her mind art books, fiction titles, and the commissioning of artists for *Puffin Story Book* covers. Others commented on how she was always ready to take an interest in other people's concerns, even if it meant joining in the tea-party of a lone five-year-old visiting Allen Lane's home Silverbeck. She had a scatty, dotty air, and at the same time she terrified her underlings with her tremendous competence.

A profound creative streak in Frost's character equipped her well for dealing with the writers and artists and other creative personalities that passed through the firm. Privately she indulged a penchant for flea-markets, Oxfam shops and period clothing. Her colleague, Tanya Schmoller remembers seeing forty pairs of shoes of every description lining the bedroom walls in her Hammersmith flat. Frost was also a member of the Chelsea Art Club, and later in life she exhibited her own paintings – 'attractive pastel things', some influenced by the Uruguayan artist Figari – in local art shows. She was instantaneously popular with the Modern Painter crowd. She had the depth and range to understand the needs of artists and writers; and a knack for combining familiarity with professionalism. But it was her humour that was the main pillar of her success: she was able to win over people like Douglas Cooper (the author of *Paul Klee* who frightened Kenneth Clark so much that he only dealt with him through an intermediary). Ivon Hitchens, Sutherland, John Summerson, and other artists would continue to drop Frost kind notes even after their involvement with Penguin had ceased.

One might guess that it was Frost's sensitive, creative side that facilitated the morbid aspect of her character. Her collapse in 1941 was a sign of things to come. There are moments in her letters – usually humorous, tactful, patient, reposed – when pain and bewilderment flare up out of the text. 'Can't you see I am doing my best against all odds?' she seems to implore, 'why such generous heapings of criticism?' Her chilly name belied a deeply sensitive soul. At times she fell ill through overwork, and an inability to put Penguin aside, even for a few days. Her doctors urged her to let go, as if Penguin were an unhealthy addiction. Even as an old woman, long retired, Frost would follow every move of Penguin obsessively. Her personal files (now in the Bristol archive) contain thick wads of yellowed newspaper cuttings about every artist and every author that ever graced a Penguin page and whose careers she had helped launch. In 1960, the combination of her sensitivity and her single-minded fixation with Penguin – a mixture that served Penguin so well – proved to be her tragic flaw. Years of overwork, underpay and lack of acknowledgement culminated in a mental breakdown, after which Frost was compelled to leave the firm she had been so instrumental in building.

In summer, 1942, working side by side with Kenneth Clark, Frost was in top spirits: full of the war effort and Penguin idealism. The challenge of co-ordinating *The Penguin Modern Painters* appealed to her artistic side and she threw herself into the project with the energy and abandon of youth. For the present she managed the series; she tended to the financial and practical arrangements while Clark saw to aesthetic considerations. Before the first four issues were published, her role would extend to encompass matters of style and content, format and the selection of pictures. Frost was rarely seen in Harmondsworth. She whizzed about between the eccentric artists and the stalwart printers, the verbose writers, the laconic photographers, and the Lords and Ladies and provincial galleries that kindly offered to loan a painting for reproduction. When paintings could not be sent for photographing she travelled across England to the homes of collectors with a photographer in tow. Considering that contributors of paintings included people like E. Sackville-West, Stephen Spender, Michael Sadler and Viven Leigh, the existence of Lane's right-hand woman was not untouched by glamour. Penguin footed the bill for many of Frost's dinners and luncheons with some of England's top pundits, authors and artists. Amidst the excitement, she managed to keep a thousand sundry details aloft in her mind at once. Her diligence paid off and by the end of 1943, she already had in hand many of the proofs for *Matthew Smith, Frances Hodgkins, William Nicholson, John Piper*, and *Edward Burra*, as well as those for the first four volumes.

At the outset of negotiations with contributors, the matter of fees and contracts had to be dealt with. Lane had offered Clark £50 per book as his editor's fee and decreed that each of the authors would likewise be paid £50. The painters were to be paid £100, but they also had to provide Allen Lane with a painting, free of charge, as part of the agreement. Most of the artists recognised the free publicity and wonderful boost to their prestige the monographs promised, and happily arranged for Lane to take his pick of their work. However, some artists were less enthusiastic about the exchange. 'I am sure the matter of giving a painting to Allen Lane will arrange itself,' Matthew Smith wrote curtly. 'I suppose not having the pleasure of Mr Lane's acquaintance has made me look on it merely as a commercial transaction.' Fortunately for Lane, Frost was an artful diplomat and his art collection would end up owing a lot to Frost's knack for the well timed and pleasant phrase.

After the contracts were written up, Frost faced the all-consuming task of tracking down paintings, vetting reproductions, and looking after details like captions and credits. Between November 1942 and January 1943, she installed herself at the National Gallery, partly to be able to consult with Clark, and partly because the Gallery had, arguably, the best photography department in London. The Gallery became a convenient holding place for paintings on loan from private individuals.

Before Frost could gather the artwork together, so that it could be photographed and sent off to Sedgwicks for proofs, Kenneth Clark had to select which paintings would best represent the artist. It was no straightforward matter. Was it necessary to include representative examples from all stages of an artist's career? Should the pictures be arranged chronologically, thematically or aesthetically? Clark allowed himself to be guided more by instinct than formula. 'The proper procedure is for authors to choose pictures they want photographed, send the list to me, and I then hand it on to the photographer block maker,' he explained to Lane. 'Some authors I am allowing to choose the reproductions, as they are working in collaboration with the artists and know what will reproduce well. Others, who are primarily men of letters and not art critics, are letting me choose the reproductions for them.' Clark later modified the lists according to the reproducibility of works, or his own preferences. If, in the *Matthew Smith* volume, 'the wriggly [nude] with fat shiny hips' followed too many other nudes 'with overpowering effect', one of the offending pictures would subsequently be switched with a flower painting. If there was a painting Clark admired, he would flatter the artist until they agreed to his suggestion. 'Could we not include the very beautiful landscape with a gate post and the full moon which was bought for the Tate at our last meeting?' he wrote to Paul Nash. 'The first plate will be in colour and should be a smasher... so it may be that it will be out of chronological order.'

Clark soon realised that given the scope of the books and the audience they were meant for, it was going to be impossible to provide a comprehensive picture of the artists or their works. A letter to Nash, who wished for his pictures to be divided into eight chronological sections corresponding to phases in his life, reveals Clark's editorial approach:

> I am full of gratitude and admiration for the great pains which you and Herbert Read have taken to make this book a complete and logical exposé of your work, and I am anxious that the series shall be as well done as possible; but after all it is only a popular series, intended to attract people with little or no previous knowledge of modern painting. No doubt many other books on your work will appear in the course of time admitting of a fuller and more systematic treatment, and so personally I do not think it worth scrapping... attractive examples [of your work] in the interests of logic.

The books were to be seductive and entertaining. Foremost, Clark wanted to impress the public with the most precious pieces the artists had on offer.

The enormity of the task of gathering together artwork during wartime is hard to fathom. Many of the paintings were scattered around the countryside, or on loan to the British Adult Educational Society or Lady Clark's British Restaurants scheme. Paul Nash had an exhibition at the National Gallery which made it easy for Frost to have a good portion of his work photographed, but other cases were not so simple: many collectors had sent paintings on tour to the US where they felt they would be safer during the war. In the worst cases, the artists themselves had no idea to whom they had sold their paintings in the first place.

A single example suffices to illustrate the challenge Frost underwent. In 1942, in search of Duncan Grant's painting *The Ass*, Frost found herself being batted around between several if not all of Roger Fry's six spinster sisters. The painting of a donkey, revealing Russian-inspired hatch-work, was considered essential for the volume: in 1914, it had represented one of Grant's strongest paintings to date, and introduced a theme he would return to in later work. Roger Fry had bought the piece when it was first exhibited at the Alpine Club Gallery in 1914, but he had since died and no one knew for certain where the painting was housed. Frost first contacted Isabel Fry, who informed her that the painting resided with Agnes Fry in Somerset, advising however, that in any event she should 'not lightly recommend the sending of such a large canvas by rail'. Undaunted, Frost then contacted the deaf Agnes Fry, who also claimed she hadn't seen the painting, but that the activist, Margery Fry, might have it since she had shared house with Roger. Further inquiries led Frost back to the implacable Isabel Fry who concluded, rather unhelpfully, that she believed she might have the painting, but if so, it was certainly hidden under a large stack of furniture, and she would 'very much prefer not to undertake or even attempt the search'. Through bull-headed perseverance, Frost discovered that the painting actually belonged to Helen Anrep, Roger Fry's second wife, who believed that it was 'at present on tour in Canada or America', but that she thought Margery Fry might have a photograph. After futher dead ends and dubious leads, Frost found her painting and it appears as plate 8 in the volume. If we consider that Frost embarked on similar searches for dozens of paintings, her achievement appears all the more remarkable.

Another obstacle presented itself in regard to paintings belonging to the War Artists collection. The Publications Division at the MoI was opposed to the reproduction of images that had already been published in the OUP books and felt that at the very least the OUP should be consulted on the issue. Eventually they agreed to allow paintings by Paul Nash, Graham Sutherland and Henry Moore to be reproduced, but requested that publication of the volumes on Bawden and Ardizzone be delayed until 'the new OUP Series has had its market'. Next the Photographic Division of the MoI got wind of the Penguin series and decided to invoice Penguin for the use of prints of all the images from their collection. Concerned with the quality of the MoI prints, Frost had already arranged for new photographs to be taken from the original artwork by Penguin's photographers, so the fee wasn't fair. In the end, Penguin had to pay the MoI the significant sum of 10/6 for each of the pictures, for nothing more than the honour of reproducing them.

Frost unhappily discovered that returning paintings could be as tricky as procuring them. In November 1943, Rothenstein, then director of the Tate, wrote reprovingly to Frost:

> The Trustees of this Gallery agreed to bring up works by Burra from one of our country refuge houses especially in order to be able to enable them to make reproductions; and subsequently agreed to allow them to be removed from the Gallery by Messrs. Sedgwick. More than a month has now passed since these works were removed. I must now write to point out that these actions of the Board represent a considerable concession on their part, and that they cannot contemplate the pictures in question being retained indefinitely.

The paintings were promptly returned, but not without a few missing frames to embitter Rothenstein's pen. Other lenders exhibited a great deal more patience, especially in view of the tremendous delays in returning work. As one collector of Ben Nicholson's work politely noted, in 1946: 'It is a little over two years since the painting was dispatched to the company for this purpose [of making reproductions] and after this rather considerable lapse of time I should be very glad to have it returned.'

★

The subject of printing techniques in the 1940s might comprise a volume of its own. With current technology, good quality reproductions are taken for granted. It is hard to imagine a time when colours were, at best, approximations of the original artwork and reproductions depended largely on the interpretive skill of the block-maker and the printer. Aware of the difficulties she faced, Frost solicited the support of R.B. Fishenden, Penguin's technical editor for the *King Penguin* series, as well as the editor of the *Penrose Annual of the Graphic Arts*. Fishenden had made the subject of printing a life study and was widely accepted as one of the foremost authorities on printing design and colour-printing technique. But even he stumbled when it came to interpreting the abstract and modernist creations of some of *The Penguin Modern Painters*. 'I wish I could understand what the artist is aiming to express,' he wrote to Frost, regarding Henry Moore's *Landscape with Figures*. Another time he complained, 'frankly the nudes do not look right to me but there is no telling what Matthew Smith's ideas are'. Fishenden's main concern was the selection of suitable works for black-and-white reproduction, to which end he nagged Clark and Frost: 'Anyone experienced in the limitations inevitable in monochrome reproduction would appreciate the difficulty and would select subjects which would retain their form in single colour reproductions.'

One ball of fire who ensured that Penguin lived up to its own standards, was the artist Paul Nash. What comes out in personal reminiscences of Nash, and in his letters to Penguin, is his superabundant energy. As Rothenstein wrote in the second volume of his three-part survey, *English Modern Painters:*

> Nash was one of those [artists] who was constantly occupied with his work. It was not that he drew or painted for more hours at a stretch than others, but he was interested in every possible aspect of his work. When he was not drawing or painting he would photograph some subject likely to be of use in a composition, or he would study some object he had found – a twisted piece of wood, a stone worn into a fantastic shape, the skeleton of a leaf – which might serve a similar purpose; he would project albums of his works, plan for exhibitions or reproductions, or he would plan the formation or actions of groups of fellow artists... With him the living of life and the pursuit of his profession were inseparably fused.

When Nash worked as a War Artist during the First World War, he left to draw the battlefields after breakfast and returned home at dinner, only to work on his drawings late into the night. Still he had time to write to his wife long, impassioned letters, containing imagery even more vivid than that found in his drawings. When he wasn't absorbed in his art, he was furthering his career; and he approached these two complementary aspects of his life with endless passion and enthusiasm.

With such a nature, it is little surprise that Nash's commitment to the quality of his reproductions bordered on the obsessive. It is also entirely understandable. From his experience as a book illustrator before the war, Nash knew that the greater the involvement of the artist in the printing process, the closer the prints would be to the artist's original vision.

In 1932, Nash published an odd little volume called *Room and Book*. Half of it is dedicated to decorating – furniture and aesthetics; the other half is about books – covers, pattern papers, and block-making. The strange mixture reflects Nash's eccentric personality. It also points to a preoccupation with both experimental and applied arts that was much more common amongst Nash's generation of artists than it is today. In the concluding chapter on 'modern processes in illustration' Nash offered advice to the budding illustrator, but also disclosed something of his approach to working with Penguin: 'The better way is for the artist to cajole the publisher and printer into a friendly conspiracy. If he is able to show a knowledge of inks, papers and types this will gain the printer's respect and slightly frighten the publisher. The artist should then have the situation in hand.' On another occasion, in the 1936 *Penrose Annual*, he wrote about the problem of colour reproduction:

He [the artist] does not expect, if he is wise, to find his picture matched colour for colour; but he does require, for instance if his painting is cool, that he will be given the same temperature in the reproduction... The most usual difference which the engraver's proof reveals is in this matter of temperature. Being a 'cold' painter I am particularly sensitive in this respect and I must confess that in all my experience I have never been spared the necessity of pointing out to the engraver that his print is too hot.

Paul Nash was indeed concerned about the temperature of the reproductions in the Penguin book. 'I do most earnestly beg someone capable of dealing with the problem to get down to the business of temperature,' he wrote to Frost. 'It is because almost all these prints are hot instead of cool that they entirely miss my colour and therefore distort the reproduction. There is no reason why this should be, surely? Could I "see" anyone if I was in London soon. I suppose all prints have to be on the white clay paper.'

Patiently, Frost henceforth met with Nash regularly. He was adamant and impossible to please, but she profited from his knowledge and quickly became well versed in the printing process, learning to walk the tightrope between quality and expediency:

I think we have discovered the solution to your general objection about the over-warm tones of your prints and that it is by printing an additional grey over the whole thing, including the surround, which has the general effect of softening and drawing the tones together... Of course if we do it it will be necessary to run the grey throughout the books, including the half-tones, and I am getting the blockmakers to pull up one or two to see what the effect will be.

The effect was, to Nash's mind, a complete failure. 'Your colour proofs just arrived,' he wrote. 'If there is one thing I am positive about it is that only one plate is improved by the grey tint and that is *Totes Meer.* The rest are destroyed as it deprives them of their one essential characteristic, luminosity. Please on no account proceed with such a disastrous expedient. I prefer the other efforts crude as many of them seem. I have suggested light printing, rather 'under strength' but I am not sure this is practicable.'

Frost badgered the printers into a host of experiments until they arrived at an effect that suited Nash. In the end, Frost drew on her natural charm to encourage the artist to approve proofs: 'Incidentally, don't you think that *Totes Meer* is greatly improved?' she wrote winningly. 'Candidly both Sir Kenneth and I feel it to be so much better than the National Gallery postcard.'

Despite Frost's administerings, Nash remained exercised about reproductions even after the book came out. 'Miss Frost has just sent me an advance copy of my Penguin book of pictures,' he informed Lane. 'It is an excellent general effect but I am rather sad to find that by comparison to the colour printings [my paintings] ultimately lose their brilliance. Have I had a freak copy or was this inevitable? The loose sheets sent just previously were so good.' Nash admitted in a later letter that he had over-reacted. 'I am abnormally sensitive to shades of quality and am largely detested in consequence.' Nash, however, wasn't alone in finding the Penguin plates problematic however; his close friend and colleague Oliver Simon wrote comparing the reproductions to those of the Curwen Press, noted for its quality printing:

It would not be appropriate for me to be writing on Curwen Press notepaper without raising a query. Surely the excellently printed colour plates are not facsimiles but interpretations. Should this not be stated in the introduction or imprint? Poor isolated virgins in Burton on Trent who hardly see a CEMA exhibition might be misled.[20]

Between meetings with Nash and other fastidious artists, Frost sent off dozens of queries regarding the proper measurements and dates of the pictures. It was all very well if the picture was in hand and the artist had scribbled the date on the back, but if a print was being used, rather than the original, it was difficult to procure correct measurements, and, more often than not, the artist hadn't remembered when he painted the work. 'Some of the dates I cannot exactly remember and have therefore added 'about', but I think they are not far wrong,' wrote Grant in 1944. 'Your sketch reminds me perfectly well of the picture *Provençal Landscape*. I have dated it as near as I can.' Some artists were vaguer than others: 'I wonder if you'll be able to coax any dates

20. Pat Gilmour, *Artists at Curwen: A Celebration of the Gift of Artists' Prints from the Curwen Studio* (London: Tate Gallery, 1977), 50.

out of Burra?' Rothenstein sceptically wrote to Lane. Edward Burra proved to be characteristically offhand about such matters: 'The list of dates seems near enough to me as I always forget them & don't remember to what they refer! Nothing is signed and they never have any dates.'

Of all the authors the vivid John Betjeman was probably the most apprehensive about his text: 'I have a hunch that Sir K will think it is no good. Then I will have to rewrite it. As I have no pride, I don't mind rewriting again and again. But you may mind waiting. So blame Sir K not me, if this happens.' Betjeman, who owed to Clark the fact that his talents were not wasted during the war, had good reason to stay on the right side of his powerful ally. But his fears were unfounded.

A few months later, he wrote ecstatically to Frost: 'Both John [Piper] & K. Clark have seen the alterations. So now we can all go ahead, swing together, heave the lead, man the foc'sle, clear the docks, pipe all hands &c.' However, it took Frost to put the finishing touches on the text and to gently guide Betjeman where he seemed to be going astray. 'I quite agree,' Betjeman wrote Frost in November, 1943, 'the implications of the first paragraph are terrifying – it all comes of living in Holy Ireland – I will alter it.'

Despite the war, unco-operative collectors, worrisome authors and artists who kept their heads in the clouds, Frost and Clark somehow moved the first four volumes to publication. *Henry Moore* and *Graham Sutherland* seem to have been printed in 1943, since first editions are dated as such, although they were not released until 1944 when the remaining two were completed. Nash's book took longer, but in January 1944, Eunice Frost was at last able to predict that the final printing of *Paul Nash* would take place in February, a forecast which proved correct.

PAPER AND PROPAGANDA

BEFORE we investigate how the first four books were received by the public and what the press said and which artists tore themselves to pieces with envy, it is essential to make a brief aside to talk about paper. No history of books published during the war can be complete without mentioning this subject, trite though it may sound. It was the problem of paper after all, that made Allen Lane go to desperate lengths to get the MoI to back his publishing ventures, and it was paper that made so many publishers turn to wartime themes to extract extra allocations from the Stationery Office.

A good source for information about paper is Hugh Barty-King's book, *Her Majesty's Stationery Office, The story of the first 200 years, 1786-1986.* The annual consumption of paper in the UK throughout the 1930s was around 3.75 million tons, of which about a third went into newspapers. During the war some of this supply was siphoned off for use in bombs and shell parts, and 'as a timber substitute in the construction of ships and aircraft'[21] An enormous quantity of paper was taken for the printed leaflets dropped over enemy and enemy-occupied territories. There were also millions of ration books of food, clothing and petrol coupons that needed printing and the government had turned its hand to producing handbooks on Air Raid Precautions. These were produced in millions, as were 'other topical publications designed to help the civilian population live through a war that was affecting them as no other had ever done.' As a result of all these inroads on supplies, shortages of paper for ordinary publishing lasted well beyond the end of the war.

The restrictions had implications for Penguin's future. In September 1939, the government instituted economy measures for paper rationing: each publishing firm was allocated 60 per cent of the paper they had used in the twelve months from September 1938 to September 1939. The terms could not have been more in Penguin's favour, if Lane had drawn them up himself. In late 1937 Allen Lane had started publishing a series of *Specials* – topical books dealing with world affairs – which had satisfied 'the craving for political enlightenment which millions of people felt at that time'.[22] Their success was tremendous, and Penguin's sales during the period the government would use to calculate paper allocations outshone those of any other publisher. This wasn't the only trump card in Penguin's hand. With characteristic

21. Valerie Holman, 'Art Books Against the Odds: Phaidon in England' 1938-1950, *Visual Resources* 15, no. 3 (1999), 322

22. *Penguins, A Retrospect, 1935-1951* (Harmondsworth: Penguin, 1951), 9.

foresight, Lane had moved his publishing house out of central London at the end of 1937 to Harmondsworth. He thereby avoided the inconvenience of moving during the war when air-raids forced so many publishers to leave and the bomb fires devastated paper supplies and stock. Stanley Unwin, another publisher, was not quite so fortunate: in his memoirs he remembers the shock of losing 1,400,000 books with a single bomb.[23]

Despite these restrictions, there were ways a publisher could cajole extra paper out of officials, and Lane became an expert: 'He seldom enjoyed himself more than when using his charm to gull some stony-faced official into believing that it was he who had first dreamed up a gracious concession which would allow to Penguin an advantage that had at first seemed unwarrantable.'[24] Paper was made available to the Stationery Office for war-related publishing, and the Paper Controller was awarded powers to give any printer directions and to fix their remuneration. This aggravated commercial publishing houses, who, as Barty-King relates, scolded it for entering the field of general publishing which was 'not one of the functions for which the Office was created'. However, it also meant that if a project seemed war-worthy, patriotic or morale-boosting, paper could be found.

23. Sir Stanley Unwin, *The Truth about a Publisher, an Autobiographical Record* (London: George Allen & Unwin, 1960), 131.

24. Quoted in Steve Hare, *Penguin Portrait* (London: Penguin Books, 1995), 96.

Penguin published so much that could fit into this category, that Lane's relations with the Paper Controller bordered on the idyllic. Not the least of his projects was the Forces Book Club – which Lane proposed to the War Office in 1941. The idea was to produce books in huge quantities for the edification and light reading of soldiers at the front. Since W.E. Williams was also the Director of the Army Bureau of Current Affairs, Lane had less difficulty getting the notion approved by the appropriate authorities and by October 1942, ten titles a month were being sent out to soldiers in runs that it was hoped would eventually reach 75,000. As a consequence of this agreement, Penguin would procure an extra allocation of sixty tons of paper a month, which by war standards was exorbitant.

These contracts not only gave Allen Lane the edge over other publishers, they also freed up paper for commercial publications, like *The Penguin Modern Painters*. Despite the good wartime paper supply, however, there is reason to believe that Lane enlisted Clark to secure further concessions to get the virtually unobtainable glossy art paper on which the reproductions in the series are printed. Clark, after all, held the unfashionable view that art could be a beneficial tonic in times of war, and he had written to the Paper Controller on behalf of other art books to express precisely this sentiment. It was a view that required a certain amount of boldness to assert when bombs were reducing neighbourhoods to rubble. In any event, unlike other Penguin wartime publications, the paper stock of the early *Modern Painters* remains virtually unyellowed to this day.

Whether due to a deliberate attempt to win over the authorities, or a consequence of the sensitivity of the authors to the war, *The Penguin Modern Painters* did indeed fulfil the function of benevolent propaganda. While the introductory essays at times demanded a high knowledge of culture, their tone was patriotic, sometimes breathlessly so. The reader learns that both of Duncan Grant's grandmothers were British and that his art is 'conspicuous in the history of the British School'. Paul Nash is likewise lauded as 'uncompromisingly English', and reference is made to his family link with Edward Lear, 'as English a genius as anyone could find'. Further, his art is compared with Blake's: 'No striving after "beauty of touch". It is the technique of Blake, an art of imagination and outline, of imagination given visual precision.' Betjeman wrote that John Piper takes after his father, 'a most English person', and then enumerates just what qualities comprise his Englishness:

Strongly individualistic with theories about education, so that his children were not sent to a boarding school: about religion, so that his children were left to choose their faith, or lack of it, in later life, about duty, so that, with little parental encouragement, he set himself to study the law and, by self-discipline and application, overcame obstacles, of which ill-health was not the least... Above everything he seems to have been the soul of integrity, a great respecter of confidence, a believer in the family as an essential unit, unflinchingly upright in domestic and financial affairs.[25]

As a subtle work of propaganda, this piece was exemplary.

It was to Lane's advantage that the British Council regarded *The Penguin Modern Painters* as legitimate propaganda. When the series was published, John Fisher from the British Council's Press Department sent out a memo in the British Council's London Letter to '230 Editors, Information Officers and other centres of distribution in Allied, Neutral and Empire territories'. Under the heading 'Popularising Modern Painters', the memo read: 'In spite of the many difficulties facing British publishers to-day, the Penguin organisation, which in peacetime persuaded the Englishman to cast aside his prejudice against paper-covered books by providing him with first-rate literature at 6d., is giving further evidence of its enterprise by issuing a new illustrated series of works on Britain's Modern Painters.' Special emphasis was placed on the *Battle of Britain* artist, Paul Nash:

Of [the first] four, Paul Nash is perhaps the best known to the average Englishman. His work attracted great attention in the last war when, after joining the Artists' Rifles, he was invalided home and held a small exhibition of drawings which he had made in the trenches. So much attention did his work arouse that he was made an official War Artist and returned to the Front in October, 1917.

Herbert Read, the art critic, wrote that where other artists – especially the poets and novelists – were to depict the

25. John Betjeman, *John Piper* (London: Penguin Books, 1944), 6.

psychological horrors of war, the aspect which Paul Nash revealed was the outrage on Nature: 'During this war Paul Nash has again attracted attention for his studies of the Battle of Britain, when he succeeded in combining reportage with a vivid imagination.'

Lane's ability to produce benign propaganda and his economy with paper ensured the munificence of the Paper Controller throughout the war.

RECEPTION

WHILE Frost, Clark and Lane were moving paintings about and cajoling printers and artists, collectors and paper suppliers, the Penguin salespeople – 'travellers' as they were known – traversed England in order to get advance orders for the monographs. They did not always meet with sympathy. In early March 1944, the irascible Paul Nash entered Alden's bookshop on Broad Street in Oxford to discover a beleaguered Penguin traveller desperately trying to sell the series to a shop manager. 'To my dismay,' Nash reported to Lane, 'they were turned down at once.' Nash immediately picked a fight with 'the wooden-faced gorgon responsible', but the bookshop manager explained to him that they would never be able to sell the series because 'mostly they were pictures of the Blitz and such was a drug in the market'. 'I wonder whether you are aware of such comical complications,' Nash inquired. Lane replied: 'It is very curious that the orders taken for the first four volumes in the series are very much better in Cambridge than in Oxford. I had not realised that Alden's had turned them down altogether, but I will have a word with our traveller when he is next in.'

Expectations like that of the 'wooden-faced gorgon' who envisioned yet more pictures of the Blitz, made the books when they came out in April 1944, a refreshing surprise. The books were landscape format – the size of two Penguin paperbacks. Their covers were two-tone, white and a golden yellow, with the name of the painter in black and a dancing penguin. Inside were engaging introductions and thirty-two prints of top quality in both black and white and colour; best of all, each volume cost only two and sixpence. As Paul Nash wrote to Clark: 'Apart from being a very interesting gallery of pictures at an incomprehensible price, it shows what can be done & it is a far reaching blow struck for the artist and the people at one and the same time.' The 'people' seemed to agree: by the end of April, 1944 Allen Lane could write to Ben Nicholson: 'We had to scale down our orders from the trade and even then our first printing is now exhausted.'

In April, Lane organised a Penguin Painters' Luncheon for the participants in the first four volumes. Clark did not appear, eliciting 'a noticeable sigh of disappointment' from the other guests, and his apology to Lane was characteristically brief: 'I was very sorry that owing to a miscalculation I was unable to come to your luncheon after all.' Duncan Grant also missed the 'lovely luncheon'. Nash made up for the absences with some bombastic speech-making, in which he congratulated everyone on the success of the books and declared to

Lane 'how immensely valuable' he regarded the project. 'Personally,' he announced, 'I would express my thanks to every participator.' It was tactful of Nash to save his disappointment over the quality of some of his reproductions for another occasion.

Clark's absence may well have been connected with his doubts about his position as the editor. Just as he had once told Frost not to put his name on the volumes as the editor before publication, afterwards he remained reluctant to accept any kudos. Around the day of the lunch party, he sat down in his office at the National Gallery and composed a series of letters to Lane and Frost and Paul Nash. 'It seems to me most unjust that your name should not appear as editor instead of mine, and I should be glad if this could be done,' he explained to Frost, 'but perhaps Alan Lane [sic] may feel that as a member of his firm you must remain anonymous.' In his letters to Paul Nash and Lane he echoed these sentiments, adding to Lane, 'the credit for [*The Penguin Modern Painters*'] good qualities must go entirely to Miss Frost, who has put an immense amount of energy into them and has been wonderfully patient with the artists. I only wish that her name could appear as editor instead of mine.'

Clark's unexpected praise touched and flattered Frost, but Lane was unnerved. Clearly Clark's commitment was waning, and Lane feared losing the patron's support, not to mention the use of his name. A month later, when Clark flatly refused his editorial fee, stating, 'the greater part of the work has been done by Miss Frost', Lane found himself at a loss. The issue was resolved to everybody's satisfaction a few days later when Clark suggested that he and Frost share the fee. Still, some encouragement was in order, and Lane promptly wrote: 'I feel that you are belittling the work you have done on *The Penguin Modern Painters*, as without you the venture would not have been possible.'

Sir Kenneth Clark wasn't the only individual who recognised that Frost was the driving force behind the series. A flurry of letters from artists arrived congratulating her. Edward Burra, always sweet and supportive, wrote: 'I saw some of the first batch in a book shop & they looked very nice I thought.' Frances Hodgkins expressed awe at Frost's achievement in wartime conditions: 'I have nothing but highest praise for the already published Modern Penguins... I do indeed realise your all but insuperable difficulties that have been so brilliantly overcome.' Paul Nash outdid everyone by giving Frost a painting, which delighted her: 'I did hope to thank you personally for your gift when I saw you in London could we have arranged it, but as it did not work out, I must thank you by letter. It was very charming and particularly so that you thought of doing it for me.'

Meanwhile, in England's incestuous and ego-ridden art world, there were certain grumbles to be heard. Ben Nicholson, for one, felt envious when the first instalment of *The Penguin Modern Painters* came out – partly his career continued to crawl along, and partly because he was unsympathetic to the aims of some of the other artists; it was he, after all, who had ruthlessly expurgated all figurative artists from the Seven and Five Society in the 1930s. The Constructivist sent congratulations to Lane but reserved more bilious comments for closer associates. The most cutting were directed at his staunchest supporter Herbert Read for his introduction to the Paul Nash volume: 'You do these appreciations of an artist's work terribly well,' he observed coldly, 'but a lot of it is an act of friendship rather than sound criticism. I think you give him a scale which he simply does not possess.' Nicholson admitted Nash was a master water-colourist, but denigrated his skill as an oil-painter: 'he is completely insensitive & hasn't the dimmest idea of how to handle the medium'. It wasn't only Nash's technique however, that was at fault. 'That *Soul visiting the Mansions of the Dead*,' moaned Nicholson, 'surely it is an appalling piece of sissy sentimentalism?' The painting Nicholson referred to is indeed rather dire. But what must have been hurtful to Read was the charge of nepotism, which could equally have been applied to the critic's stalwart championship of Nicholson's own work. Nicholson's sneers were also extended to Graham Sutherland, whose oak trees, he said in a letter to John Summerson, reminded him of 'Aunt Agatha's bowels'. The frustrated artist also disparaged Henry Moore's recent work as 'more or less meaningless as enduring ideas'. So much for expansive, enlightened artists. But the mockery went in both directions. In late November, 1944, Edward Bawden and William Coldstream – then stationed as War Artists in Rome – shared a laugh at the puritanical commitment to 'advanced' art as practised by Nicholson's circle. 'At tea this afternoon,' Bawden wrote to his wife, '[Coldstream] gave a wicked imitation of a prayer-meeting led by Herbert Read and Ben and Barbara [Nicholson-Hepworth] praying with Salvation Army gusto, confessing their sins of representation, and asking the good Lord to make them abstract and advanced.'

The publication of the first four volumes unleashed more pre-war art world antagonism in a review in *The New Statesman and Nation*, written by the Bloomsbury artist Clive Bell. 'Maybe Graham Sutherland is not a painter,' he announced derisively, 'Maybe he is something else – a mythopoeist his encomiast seems to suggest. Anyhow, if Giotto, Rubens, Chardin, Constable and Cézanne were painters, it is arguable that Sutherland is not one.' As for the authors, Bell began his appraisal pessimistically: 'In my opinion one only has quite succeeded in writing a critical and exegetic essay on the painting, or rather drawing, of the particular artist assigned to him.' Ironically, Bell's hard-headed review isn't written clearly enough for us to know which author he approved of, unless it was Herbert Read who sensibly 'allowed the artist to speak for himself' by using extensive quotes. Of the other volumes, Bell provided rather mixed reviews: in Raymond Mortimer's essay, 'the pre-eminent quality of his artist's painting remains undefined'; Mr Grigson 'enlivens his page with irrelevancies'; and Mr Sackville-West admires his hero too strongly:

> To passionate admiration much shall be forgiven; nevertheless, I think he makes him look silly when he says 'here, surely, is a complementary vision' [Moore's figures in a Sutherland landscape] 'that takes us back, in it noble adequacy and completeness, to the stupendous world of Piero della Francesca'.

Despite such reservations, Clive Bell advised people of taste 'to subscribe forthwith for the series'.

In some respects, mixed reviews like Bell's which actually engaged with the art and the ideas behind it, were preferable to wholly positive reviews. *The Manchester Guardian* review was glowing, but sounded like it had been lifted from Penguin's press release:

> Between the modern painter and the ordinary man a great and regrettable gulf has hitherto seemed permanently fixed. To bridge that gulf – or rather to dispel that illusion – is the supremely worth-while purpose which Sir Kenneth Clark has undertaken, and brilliantly begun to achieve, as general editor of *The Penguin Modern Painters*... Each artist's work is interpreted by a sympathetic critic who is himself a writer of repute... Best of all, half the reproductions (on pages of twice the normal Penguin size) are in colour of a quality never before approached at anything like the price.

Likewise, *Current Literature* had little to say beyond the assertion that the series would 'fully maintain the Penguin reputation for value for money'.

Unsurprisingly, less well-versed critics were bemused. A reviewer in *The Process Engraver's Monthly* regarded some of the abstract work as 'tentative experiments', 'curious sketches and trial trips' with little interest to anyone except fans and 'souvenir hunters'. Still, he concluded on an upbeat: 'From the artist's angle these booklets are instructive and supremely worth having; from the collector's angle they will be welcomed; and from the connoisseur's angle they will be seized upon as a basis for considerable argument.'

Press coverage extended as far afield as Penguin's distribution. There was a review in Jerusalem as well as a Swedish review published in a Stockholm magazine that no one in London art circles could understand. The *Palestinian Post* described the first four volumes as a single cross-referencing unit, while commenting 'the most powerful of the four is Henry Moore: born in 1898, the son of a Yorkshire miner, his fame as one of the world's leading sculptors began in the early 30s.' Ties between Moore and Sutherland were especially emphasised:

> If there is anything we could expect to encounter in Sutherland's mysterious and sometimes macabre landscapes it would be one of Moore's half-human figures looking at their war scenes. One might even go further: Sutherland paints devastated and deserted streets, and Moore the people sleeping quietly in tube shelters.

The review ended with a comment on the series' usefulness to people around the world: 'Those who have no chance to see the originals in English galleries will welcome these publications.' If nothing else, the broad range of comment and acclaim proved how far-reaching Penguin's arm had been in popularising English modern painters.

INNUMERABLE DELAYS

In July 1944 the Germans had started a last-ditch attempt to demoralise England with V-bombs. Several times a month Lane and Frost were required, along with the rest of the Penguin staff, to act as night-time fire-watchers at Harmondsworth. In addition to these distractions, procuring art to photograph for the volumes remained a burden, and the challenge of producing top-quality reproductions when printers' blocks were continuously being destroyed by enemy bombs translated into severe delays for the next four Modern Painters. In autumn 1944 a rumour starting drifting around art circles that Penguin had decided to abandon the series. The rumour was entirely unfounded, of course, and the cause of the disruption in publishing had no connection with any lack of initiative on Penguin's part, but it frustrated and demoralised the artists who were anxious to see their monographs appear.

While bombs whistled overhead, a less ominous storm was brewing in Penguin's offices. At the celebratory luncheon for the first four Modern Painters in May, someone, probably Lane, introduced the tantalising idea of including photographs of the artists in the introductions of future volumes. The proposal was applauded by all, especially the artists present who fancied seeing their own portraits in reprints of their volumes. They all referred to the public appeal of picturing the artist (as if egotism played no part in their enthusiasm), and urged Lane and Frost to go ahead with the plan. Lane was undeterred by the fact that Clark had rejected the idea earlier and he wrote telling him the results of the discussion. Clark responded with what he admitted were 'certain conventional objections', but admitted that photos would have 'great popular appeal'. 'To tell the truth,' he confessed, 'I myself am always interested to see portraits of writers or painters whose work I like; so I suppose my objection to it is slightly hypocritical.' Clark added as a postscript: 'Also I see great technical objections in the make up.'

The debate escalated when other editors at Penguin declared that getting the series out at all was already a miracle, and the portrait would add just another hitch in the long series of delays. As always, Lane had his way, and Frost wrote to Nash that, 'although we had some battles here... it has been decided, by a majority of one vote that in future volumes we propose to devote the entire space at present covered by type on the first column of the second page of text to a photograph of the artist.'

It fell to the over-worked Frost to chase artists for photographs, who didn't help matters with their relentless vanity. 'Here at last is the only portrait I feel I can bear,' wrote an elderly Paul Nash. 'It has an impersonal mark-like air which I prefer to other more 'human' visages. It is rather 'early' but I don't see why I should present my ravaged looks for the sympathy or disquiet of the Public.' Frost suggested gently, 'I suppose you quite emphatically decided on using an early portrait and I think if it turns out satisfactorily enough and we use it, we had better add a date. Don't you?' Meanwhile Edward Bawden who was in a twist about the whole business sent in a selection of pictures: 'I hate the thought of an artistic photograph which would camouflage the uglier of my features by throwing them in mysterious shadow. The BBC took quite a straightforward likeness without the least frilliness... I do hate having to face that nasty little box with the evil eye!' Bawden quickly changed his mind about the BBC snapshot, writing: 'I like the one taken with Antony Gross in Cairo – do please use this one. It is quite easy to cut the photograph in half. I look about the age of 18 which pleases me, & I do like the painted background. The BBC photograph is too soulful.' In 1947, the portraits were dropped. Little explanation was given except in a letter from Frost to Mrs Nash: 'It is not going to be possible to use the photograph in the way you suggested, as it was necessary to reset the text in such a way as to make it impossible to have a photograph at all.'

The delays incurred by the war irked some writers since it led to problems with the texts. Like several of the authors, Clive Bell had rushed off his introduction to the volume on Victor Pasmore promptly in 1942, directly after Clark had invited him to join the series. Two years later, there was no sign of the book, and Pasmore had moved into an unprecedented phase in which his works verged on abstraction. Frost received from Bell the sort of dejected letter she became accustomed to during the uncertain days when delays and hardships were rife:

> I shall be very glad to correct a revised proof; more than that I shall not attempt. To do so would be to rewrite the essay. That, I think, is what Pasmore would like me to do, and I quite understand his feeling. In the last two years his art has made great progress and changed considerably. But I cannot write a new essay; neither would you agree to it if I were willing. I must say that, in my opinion, it would have been better, and fairer to the artist, if you had not asked me to write till you were in a position to publish within (say) six months. A great deal is bound to happen to a young and growing painter in two years. However, times are difficult; and anyhow there's no scuse in crying over spilt milk. Only I could wish my share in the book had been as good as it might have been. If you find it unsatisfactory, as you will, since much of it is out of date, I trust you will have the justice to lay the blame on the appropriate back, i.e. not mine.

When the volume was finally published in 1945, Bell's essay was even more dated, although Penguin had been able to include plates for paintings from 1943 and 1944. Most notable of these were *A Wave* (1939-44) and *The Quiet River* (1943-44)), river scenes in which an abstract or constructive quality can be discerned in the relationship of horizontals and verticals, and rectangular masses of colour. As for the introduction, a compromise was found. Bell had ended his original text with the line 'I prophesy that the art of Pasmore will not stand still'; to this he added the following postscript:

Since this Introduction was written, has been shown [sic] at the Redfern Gallery a small collection of paintings which justifies my prophecy. The progress made would in any circumstances be remarkable; in those which prevail it is extraordinary. Also it is in the right direction. As the statement becomes clearer and more confident the fog disperses; and the artist's sense of form becomes as visible as his feeling for colour has always been. *The Flower Barrow* (retouched), which hitherto had been reckoned Pasmore's masterpiece, was on view. It remains a lovely picture but it is no longer the artist's masterpiece. He has gone beyond it.

In a sense the volume was published just in time. Less than two years later, in 1947, Pasmore fully made the transition from figurative to abstract painting. The Penguin monograph forms a nice point of closure for the first half of his career.

In December 1944, Paul Nash scribbled one of his frantic postcards to Frost: 'There is a malicious rumour circulating to the effect that the first 4 have sold so badly you are not doing any more artists.' He received this reply: 'Miss Frost... would like to tell you that there is no foundation for such a rumour as you mentioned. In fact, so successful have the Modern Painters been, that we have increased the printing order on the next four to be published.' The next two, *Matthew Smith* and *John Piper*, were indeed published that month with print runs of 41,000. And by this time, 15,000 more copies of the volume on Henry Moore – replete with portrait – had been printed.

Of all the artists in the series, Matthew Smith was the only one to voice voluble objections to the introduction of his monograph. The text was by Sir Philip Hendy, who, at the time of writing, was, simultaneously, the Slade Professor of Fine Art at Oxford University, and the Director of the City Art Gallery and Temple Newsam, Leeds. Before writing the introduction, he had met Smith several times to discuss what little streams of influence had flowed (to borrow Betjeman's phrase), 'into the single river of mature production'. One would expect Hendy to have written an insightful and carefully weighted introduction to Smith's work. And most people agreed that he had.

The problem for Smith was that Hendy had focused on an issue that was sensitive to him. Smith, though in his sixties, pursued young women with what bordered on obsessiveness. It has even been suggested that he sought the company of talented womanisers like Augustus John and Jacob Epstein in order to ride to success, so to speak, on their coat-tails. His propensity for womanising, however, seemed at odds with his frail and elderly appearance. He came across as a slightly nervous man. Although Smith could be a popular party-goer, it was not uncommon for people to notice the disparity between the man with the slight figure and his luscious, lusty nudes. In his introduction, Hendy implied that Smith created vibrant sensuous canvases as a way of compensating for something he lacked himself. The underlying suggestion, at least as Smith interpreted the passage, was that Smith's paintings in some way made up for his own sexual infirmity:

Some men in their persons and their lives are just like their art, which seems to be only an extension of their personality. Smith is of the opposite kind. Spare and shy and self-deprecatory, he puts into his painting, I should say, the things which nature has not given him. His art is complementary to himself.

Smith regarded this image of himself as distorted and derided Hendy's 'pseudo-psychological' analysis of his work.[28] To be fair to Smith, his biographer, Malcolm Yorke, takes his side entirely:

If this is also a hint that [his works'] eroticism is a sublimation of a frustrated sexual drive then Hendy could not have known the artist well: at this level the works were surely yet another way of caressing and possessing his women and commemorating his intimacy with them – this is why he never sold many of them. These were the very things which nature *had* given him and the canvases were his notes of thanks.

Smith was also irritated that Hendy had neglected to mention an early struggle with an oppressive father which had been so instrumental in forming his work and life and was, he felt, the true cause of his nervousness. As a child he had lived in constant fear of his father's displeasure, who believed that 'the place of arts was in those leisure hours when the serious business of the day was over.' After much battling, the young Smith was permitted to attend the Manchester School of Art, but not until his father had telephoned the Principal and given strict instructions that his son 'was on no account to be allowed near any class-room where women were posing in a state of undress.'[29] For his part, Hendy felt that all artists have to grapple with disapproving parents, and he didn't see why Smith should be regarded as a special exception. '[Smith] complained bitterly to me and on several occasions,' Rothenstein wrote in his memoirs, 'that his family's opposition to his becoming a painter had been ignored (although he had made, he said, a special point of it in talking to Hendy), as well as the disastrous and lifelong effect of the consequent friction upon his nerves.'

The press overlooked Smith's point of contention, and instead poked holes in Hendy's description of the artist's use of colour. Hendy had asserted that Smith 'used glazes, as no other modern Englishman has managed to do, to get pure, clean, brilliant colours with the contours, too, outlined and shaded in strong hues...' It was a strange thing to say about an artist for whom a painting was finished the minute it dried. Glazing, as the artist's biographer relates, involves 'floating one layer of thin colour over another which then shows through' – a technique Smith would hardly have had the patience

28. Malcolm Yorke, *Matthew Smith, His Life and Reputation,* (London: Faber and Faber, 1997), 182.

29. Francis Halliday and John Russell, 'Biographical Note,' *Matthew Smith* (London: George Allen and Unwin, 1962).

for 'in his haste to wrestle his vision down on to the canvas.' A reviewer in *The Nineteenth Century and After* attacked Hendy's celebration of Smith's use of colour, and managed to disparage the artist at the same time: 'All critics agree that Mr Smith is a modest man, but some of them have encouraged him to exploit a pretentious manner... quality in paint is not obtained by lumping it on straight from the tube, the result is invariably poor and greasy.'[30] All the same, Hendy's introduction came to be regarded as one of the most valuable in series: *The Studio* described it as 'altogether admirable: concise, balanced and interesting'; and even Ben Nicholson, usually so ready to pour contempt, wrote fondly of the volume to his friend Margaret Gardiner: 'A v. good 'Matthew Smith' Penguin has just come. What a charming person he looks – how is it that none of us know him? Or do you?'[31] In 1962, Hendy wrote a glowing introduction to a monograph on Smith for George Allen and Unwin. He omitted any mention of the artist's delicacy, and instead focused on the sumptuousness of his paintings: 'The zest that Smith gained by this conquest of the nude was soon spilling over into still lifes and flower pictures of a new power and richness... I can think of no artist who has used flowers and fruit to express such a variety of ecstasy, from cool delight to passionate orgy.'

30. R.W. Alston, *The Nineteenth Century and After* (August 1945).

31. Margaret Gardiner, A Portrait of Ben Nicholson II, *Modern Painters* (Autumn 1989)

When it came to Betjeman's text for *John Piper, The Studio* took the stance that it did 'not come up to [Hendy's] standard', mostly because it was too biographical: 'His opening sentence: "I feel disposed, as well as more competent, to back up this book with biography rather than critical analysis" explains, in a way, this failure', explained the reviewer. 'No attempt is made to deal with controversial issues; an obvious one is Piper's preoccupation with a narrow, literary romanticism.' In truth, the latter comment was more a criticism of Betjeman than Piper. Betjeman was an admirer, friend and colleague of the artist and it was from this enviable position that he was able to take the reader through 'the books, drawings and old canvases of his house' to paint a picture of the artist's early propensities, his ancestors, how he copied stained-glass windows and loved Italian architecture as a teenager, and how, during his formative years, his family took him on camping expeditions to Sussex where they spent their days sketching. Betjeman depicted Piper, perhaps, as a man more obsessed with English churches than with ideas. And at a time when ideas in art were paramount, this tack was bound to be unpopular. The *Studio*'s review was not the only one to find fault with Piper's vision and Betjeman's celebration of it. John Piper 'tinkers with the surface of ideas', Ben Nicholson informed Margaret Gardiner '& there's an introduction by Betjeman which would go well in the gossip column of the *Ladies Home Journal*'.[32]

32. Quoted in Checkland, 227.

John Piper and *Matthew Smith* narrowly escaped an event which was to disrupt the publication schedule of *The Penguin Modern Painters* for months – and possibly years – to come. In spring 1945 the indispensable Eunice Frost took one of her protracted trips to the Penguin branch in America. Prior to the war, Lane had opened the US branch mainly as an import agency: he sent the branch books, and they sold them. The branch's expansion however, was impeded by the war: German submarines sank shipments of books, and the British government refused to extend credit for foreign investment. Within two years of the outbreak of war, it became apparent to Ian Ballantine, who had been appointed by Lane to run Penguin's New York office, that it was important that the branch become fully operational: in other words, that it produce its own books, rather than relying on uncertain imports from Britain. Ballantine left to set up Bantam at the end of the war, and Lane appointed Kurt Enoch and, later Victor Weybright, to direct the flourishing publishing programme specifically for the US audience. Frost's task was to make certain that the new company adhered to the Penguin standards which Lane guarded, some thought, too dearly.

When Frost arrived at the cramped New York premises she had to share an office with Weybright. Down the corridor were offices inhabited by toy companies and rug distributors. For months she lived out of a suitcase in the Gramercy Park Hotel. Nonetheless, she managed to recruit and train two top-rate editors, Arabel J. Porter and Donald Demarest, and enlist Saul Bellow as a temporary manuscript reader. 'Eunice Frost I dearly loved,' remembers Bellow. 'She was what some Americans in those days referred to as a six-foot dove... My task was to help her get together the first Penguin list for the USA. I was paid five dollars for every work of fiction, and ten dollars for non-fiction books. I read them most attentively and wrote lengthy reports and carried a sack of books up and down the Harlem Valley.'

Frost and her new crew rounded up hundreds of titles as candidates for reprint. As Weybright recalls in his memoirs of the period, her literary and scholarly taste, 'paved the way for my active beginning in the best Penguin tradition'.

The New York branch may have been resurrected under Frost's tutelage, but her absence threw the England office into a state of pandemonium. Lane noted, with some understatement in an office memo, 'there was in consequence a certain amount of disorganisation in our Editorial and Production Departments'. As for *The Penguin Modern Painters* series, the list of all Ardizzone's illustrations had disappeared, as well as all the data pertaining to them, collectors were disgruntled at going without their paintings for so long, and the artists and authors were once again losing hope and interest.

One day in October 1945 Clark wrote to Lane expressing his fear for the recovery of the series:

I am growing rather worried about *The Penguin Modern Painters...* The artists are becoming rather restive and authors resigned. Can anything be done to hurry things up? For example is there anyone else in your office who could take a personal interest in seeing the volumes through the press?

Lane, who was liable, as Williams remembered, 'to plunge or to hesitate', decided, after receiving Clark's anxious letter, to whisk the Burra and Pasmore volumes, which Frost had virtually completed before leaving for America, off to the printers without further commotion. As if by magic, the books, which only a few weeks before had been plates and proofs lying forgotten in storage rooms, appeared on shelves in time for Christmas. In January 1946, a reviewer in *The Listener* could remark: 'By this time the format of *The Penguin Modern Painters* series is well known... The series has become deservedly popular because of its price, excellent printing and complete lack of pretentiousness.'

The arrival of two more volumes, then, did not go unheralded by the press. The above comment prefaced a review of the Pasmore and Burra volumes, which were written by Clive Bell and John Rothenstein respectively, two of the most eminent authors in the series. In the case of both books, the reviewer took with one hand and gave with the other:

Mr Bell never quite succeeds in... describing [the artist] so that the words used could not possibly apply to any other painter... His method (and it is one at which he is expert) is to prepare the reader, by a species of pleasantly urbane causeries, for the artist's arrival and then to let the pictures explain for themselves their difference from those of, say, Degas or Bonnard. The method makes for pleasanter reading than the grimmer process of analysis.

Likewise:

Dr Rothenstein devotes half of his introduction to biographical detail and the other half to a discussion of the subject-matter rather than the flavour of Burra's highy flavoured water-colours. That is a reasonable division. And when he does tackle the flavour he can invent a pregnant phrase – 'a new rococo which has a copious and exotic grandeur and the deliquescent fantasy which belongs to dreams'. That is good descriptive writing though it does not fully suggest the sultry weight of Burra's colour or the slow-moving deliberation of his line.

On the whole, in this reviewer's estimation, both authors failed because neither of them were able to analyse the artists in detail, 'so that one could almost conjure up a mental image of the essential Burra-esque and Pasmore-esque mood without having actually seen a picture by either painter.' It was an impossibly tall order, and most would forgive Bell and Rothenstein their all too human limitations.

With *Edward Burra* and *Victor Pasmore* in the bookshops it was tempting for those at Penguin to take a breather from the series, but the fact remained that there were still at least nine more English volumes floating about in varying degrees of completion. In January, Lane advised Clark:

We have I think now caught up on all outstanding matters, and the two new titles, *Edward Burra* and *Victor Pasmore* which appeared last month, are the forerunners of an accelerated programme. They will be followed early this year by *Edward Bawden* and *Stanley Spencer*. Of the former all the blocks are made and passed by the artist. The text is set up and the book will be going on the machines during the next few weeks. Of the latter, all the colour blocks are made but there are one or two black and whites still to come.

Lane's optimism was misplaced. The Bawden and Spencer volumes indeed were published in 1946, but not until December. And it would be an additional two years before *William Nicholson, Ben Nicholson, Frances Hodgkins,* and *David Jones* finally emerged from the printers resplendent in chocolate-coloured card covers (with the exception of David Jones who wore a sophisticated greyish-blue).

The delay was especially painful for those artists whose lives had been severely disrupted by the war, and for whom a monograph represented, at the very least, a vindication of their artistic careers, and at best, an opportunity to reach a broad new audience.

One such artist was Ben Nicholson who had moved to Cornwall with his children and wife, Barbara Hepworth, to escape the Blitz. No longer was he the toast of Hampstead artists, the centre of *Circle* and the Seven and Five Society. In St Ives and later, in Carbis Bay, he was isolated, struggling to support six children, with finances so tight he had to persuade the local electrician to accept a painting in exchange for a radio.

To make things grimmer, conservative schools of art – Euston Road and Neo-Romanticism – were in the ascendancy. It was difficult not to feel an outcast. Another monograph on Ben Nicholson, proposed by a Sinhalese publisher, Tambimuttu in summer, 1944, had also not seen the light of day.[33] Meanwhile, those around him were enjoying the fruits of their labour: Faber and Faber were preparing a modest monograph on Barbara Hepworth, and a flattering biography had already been written on his father William Nicholson by his last lover Marguerite Steen, which he said made him 'physically sick' to read (mainly for its depiction of his mother as 'moody', 'indolent', and lacking 'invention').[34]

Nicholson's spirits were raised temporarily when, in the spring of 1946, John Summerson trotted down to St Ives again with the revised galley. But months later there was still no sign of publication.

Ben Nicholson's prospects, however, were hardly worse than those of his friend and colleague Frances Hodgkins, another artist in exile from London whose Penguin monograph seemed faced with interminable delays.

A typical late snapshot of Hodgkins shows her lodged under a tree with a drawing pad. She wears a thick plaid shirt, a man's cravat, and a tweed skirt. From under her homburg hat project two great tufts of white frizzy hair. Hodgkins was an old lady, more a member of William Nicholson's generation than his son's. But in spirit she belonged to the cast of middle-aged British artists, people like Ivon Hitchens, Henry Moore and Paul Nash – she had been a member of the Seven and Five Society,

33. Checkland, 231.
34. Checkland, 222.

and for a short while, of Unit One. It was her refusal to be compromised in her own craft, by convention, ambition, and least of all the marketplace, which allowed her to preserve her elasticity as an artist to the end.

Though she only bloomed late in life as an artist, Hodgkins' background was a rich tapestry of artistic experimentation and intermittent adventure. Once she spent three months stranded in a native caravan in Tetuan, Morocco, where she was besieged by bandits. After leaving her native New Zealand as a young woman, she lived on and off in Paris, and went for frequent jaunts across Europe before settling in England, where she supported herself teaching watercolour painting. The critical moment in her career occurred in her sixties, when the prominent critic Eric Newton lauded her as a painter of 'genius' after an exhibition at the Lefevre Gallery. By 1940 Hodgkins was regarded by the cultural élite as 'the most inventive colourist in England' and reviewers were likening her to Renoir and Bonnard.

Despite the acclaim, the war years were difficult for Hodgkins. Because she had never taken root for long in one place, she had collected many acquaintances in life, but few close friends to cosset her in her old age. In Corfe, where she lived in a comfortless studio, she must have felt isolated. The wartime coal shortages resulted in insufficient heating and her fingers swelled to twice their size with chilblains. What she liked to describe as 'the solace of art' became a source of pain and frustration. The constant buzz of enemy planes on their way to Bristol sapped her spirits.

To say that the Penguin monograph became one of the main pillars upon which Hodgkins balanced her hopes during the war, would not be an exaggeration, as her late letters are scattered with plentiful mentions of the volume. However, the ups and downs of the book's production made it a precarious pillar indeed. After Myfanwy Evans, the only female author in the series, interviewed Hodgkins extensively about her art and her life in July 1942, Hodgkins fretted over how she would be perceived. Her work was associated with the younger artists and few people knew her real age. She took little issue with it, but she was afraid that others would: 'On the subject of age you are dead right,' she wrote to Evans. 'I regard myself as a mature veteran not old, but ageing. In some ways finding my years more a privilege than anything else – Oh! The Drums that I have followed.' Hodgkins was also sensitive to the question of gender: as a female artist, she had struggled against a prejudice that had denied her acknowledgment all her life. It seems that, as an old woman, she feared being regarded as something of a novelty act, or at the very least, pigeon-holed by her sex. At one point, she asked Evans: 'I should like to know if my Book is included in the main group Sutherland – Piper – or something slightly different *with other women*.'

Months after the interview, Hodgkins heard that her close friend, Dorothy Selby, had handed over to Evans a bundle of her personal letters. She flew into a panic: 'I dislike intensely my private life being brought into any sort of prominence – and letters will very soon dry up at their source if letters are handed round without given permission.'[35] Hodgkins' anguish was quelled when Evans sent her the text, which she spent an entire weekend reading and rereading:

Let me congratulate you – I think it is very good – It is excellent. I call it uncanny the way you have unravelled the tangle of my life story & made it into a really lovely little grandiose Book. Not quite me – but near enough as may be – Pleasantly salted with malice – as it should be. Very readable – very credible – really d—d good by your leave... Between us, your words & my painting go well together.

To her friend, Katharine West, Hodgkins expressed her relief that Evans 'kept the artist well in front of the human being'.[36]

The appearance of the first four volumes precipitated another slump in Hodgkins' spirits. Firstly her own monograph was nowhere in sight: she had not yet even seen proofs of her own illustrations. Secondly, in the inside front covers of the first four, where future monographs were listed, her own name didn't appear. Assuming that she had been dropped from the list, she found herself not only intolerably agitated, but left with the humiliating problem of what to do with the painting she had selected for Lane as her part of the bargain. She wrote to Evans once again:

Am living on a petty plane full of troublesome jobs and doing little painting – So when you can spare the time do just drop me a line to say how you are – and what is expected of me in regard to the token picture. I do dislike this uncertainty & the intolerable sense of sin & frustration caused by an unfinished creative act. It is cumulative & in the end kills the artist. [37]

Her anguish injected a note of sarcasm into her appraisal of the first four volumes, which she genuinely admired: 'How very good indeed they are the 4 élite, elect Aristocrats – I am the happy possessor of all 4 – It should be a raging success and everyone in need of the solace of Art should have a copy.'

Evans replied assuring Hodgkins that Penguin had no intention of dropping her from the series, but the artist's pride remained bruised when she heard that she was destined for the third batch of four: 'I am feeling an outcast as well as a bit of a dam fool for caring whether I appear with the first 4 Penguins or the last four.' While she was brooding over her absent monograph, her health and spirits continued to lag. 'How vile it is all this devilry,' she said in a letter to Dorothy Selby. 'The village is stiff with troops... the motor traffic is terrific... The planes overhead bringing back the wounded from Normandy have scared all the art out of me – I simply cannot paint.'

To her credit, Evans, who was bogged down with an

35. Frances Hodgkins to Dorothy Selby, 22 December 1942, *Letters of Frances Hodgkins* (Auckland: Auckland University Press, 1993), 531.

36. Frances Hodgkins to Katharine West, 4 April 1943, *Letters of Frances Hodgkins*, 535.

37. Frances Hodgkins to Myfanwy Evans, 8 June 1944, *Letters of Frances Hodgkins*, 549

infant and the day-to-day drudgery of domestic life, did everything in her power to expedite the Penguin monograph, including marching over to Sedgwicks and interrogating the operator until he had made a list of adjustments needed to bring the illustrations up to scratch. Hodgkins, at least, expressed gratitude: 'Do believe me I have no black looks for you, on the contrary I am full of pangs & sympathy & admiration for your energy in poking up the poor photographer-printer to get on with the job "with all speed".' Now it was Myfanwy Evans' turn to feel frustrated: the operator put the job to one side and promptly forgot the whole conversation. It was many months later when Evans complained to Frost in despair: 'Now if they are so vague and stupid they can't even remember that long session I give them up.'

When the war ended, Hodgkins continued to fluctuate between buoyancy and depression, with the monograph as a main component affecting her mood: 'I have been suffering from a bit of a break down and my work, of necessity has slowed down if not actually stopped. One good thing however has emerged from the battling which is: the reappearance of Old Man Penguin not far off publishing point.'

During Frost's absence in America, one individual had taken over responsibility for *The Penguin Modern Painters*, though only in an unofficial capacity. This was the eccentric in-house editor A.S.B. Glover, who was hired by Lane in 1944 because for two years he had been writing to Penguin to point out misprints. Glover had been imprisoned as one of the few 'absolutists' during the First World War, and, as Morpurgo wrote in his autobiography, *Master of None*, he was as expert in 'Russian literature, psychoanalysis and the more obscure religions – to most of which he had been converted at some time in his life – as he was about cricket scores or bus timetables'. Glover was also a faultless proof-reader, and Tanya Schmoller fondly remembers him reading masses of galley-proofs while standing in the tube and watching them blow everywhere when the train opened its doors at a station. Art, however, was not Glover's forte, and he embraced the task of managing *The Penguin Modern Painters* with rather less enthusiasm than had the inestimable Frost.

And so the books languished.

To be fair to Glover, he was left holding the helm of an organisational shipwreck. The captain, Kenneth Clark, and the chief helmsman, Frost, had all but extricated themselves and made for distant shores. Even when Frost returned from America in April 1946, she was far too busy organising a volume on Ben Shahn in order to launch the American Modern Painter series in time for a Shahn exhibition at the Museum of Modern Art, to speed the remaining English books to press. Moreover, her remaining enthusiasm was now captured by the prospect of Cuban, Mexican and Brazilian volumes.

The aftermath of war exacerbated the chaos. In the early months of 1946, the economy was embarking on a period of restructuring, there were power shortages, and institutions were in a state of upheaval. Old members of staff were returning from abroad and expecting to find their old jobs intact. Others were leaving ad hoc wartime positions, and taking the day-to-day details of their jobs with them.

An unfortunate departure was that of Kenneth Clark who left the National Gallery. His position was filled by Philip Hendy, a more strictly conscientious and sober person. Glover hoped that the new Director would afford Penguin the same privileges at the gallery they had enjoyed with Clark: 'I need not say we should appreciate it very much if you were prepared to permit us to continue on occasion to park a picture there for a short while in the course of its travels!' he wrote. The reply, from Hendy's assistant was discouraging: 'As all our pictures have now been returned to the National Gallery, and as a considerable part of the Gallery has been damaged and is unfit for storage, we are very short of space, and [Hendy] regrets, therefore, that it will not be possible in the future for us to undertake to give temporary storage to your pictures.' Glover was then advised to collect all the paintings at the gallery immediately – a confusing task considering no one, not even Kenneth Clark's secretary, had a clue where the pictures were hiding. After much scrambling, the paintings were discovered collecting dust in one of the gallery's remote storage rooms. It was no wonder that collectors who lent works lost patience.

One monograph which posed particular problems for Glover – and whose story is telling of the effect wartime delays had on some of the books – was that on the artist David Jones. Jones was a waif-like man with large mild eyes, a languid figure and 'a pervasive quiet' about him.[38] His paintings were likewise delicate, sensitive and paradoxical, containing shifting layers of present-day landscape and ancient mythology, and blends of boldness and opalescence. Unsurprisingly, they were difficult to reproduce. Compounding the problem, unlike Paul Nash, David Jones was too mild-mannered to interject with advice to the printers on his own behalf.

During the war the photo engravers dealing with the Jones' monograph were compelled, owing to several bombings, to move location, and their material was, in the words of Glover 'reduced to a rather chaotic condition'. The Jones plates, which had already been lovingly pondered over and approved, would have to be worked on from scratch. The least happy person to hear this was Helen Sutherland, a severe looking art patron who acted as a friend and loyal supporter of many artists, poets, musicians and authors in the 1930s and 1940s. Sutherland made her home a retreat where artists might find both respite from the world and inspiration for their craft – provided they abided by her puritanical schedule. Before the war, David Jones used to settle himself quietly before a window in one of the front rooms of her rambling house and paint northern landscapes. As a self-appointed mother of the arts and an avid collector,

38. John Rothenstein, *Modern English Painters, Volume Two, Nash to Bawden* (London: MacDonald, 1984), 208.

she had in her collection a good many paintings by Jones and other British artists and was frequently called upon to loan works for the series. When she heard what had happened to the plates, she was 'horrified':

> Mr David Jones' watercolours are large & particularly frail & liable to damage – I have only just heard that someone who lent one – has received it back damaged – the glass having broke. There is no doubt that these large drawings are more frail than oil paintings & any damage I fear much more difficult to repair... I should very much prefer again to receive your Photographer or engraver here. At the moment my house is full & it will be full till about mid-May I think.

Thus admonished, Glover waited until the end of the spring whereupon he sent the Penguin photographer off to Sutherland's luxurious home in Cockley Moor. Sutherland received him at the train station and generously put him up for the night. The photographer may have felt, as Kathleen Raine did upon first visiting Sutherland, that he had entered 'a place of the imagination – some castle in Spenser... one of those places of arrival where treasures are shown to pilgrim or traveller and wounds are healed.' In this case the treasures were Miss Sutherland's famous collection of paintings by artists such as Seurat, Ben Nicholson, Courbet, and Mondrian. (She kept two Picassos, which she didn't like, in a cupboard.)[39] But it was no substitute for having the paintings in the workshop where the photo engravers and printers could test inks and colour combinations until they arrived at the most truthful reproductions. As Fishenden had noted to Frost in 1943: 'How much better it is when the engravers can have the paintings in their studios.'

In spring 1947 Jones had a complete nervous breakdown, perhaps because his nerves had never quite recovered from the trenches. The quietly complex and ethereal artist spent much of the year in a nursing home in Harrow receiving psychotherapy. As far as the monograph was concerned, it was bad timing because it meant he was unable to provide what would have been most valuable advice about the quality of his reproductions. In 1949 when the book appeared (a full six years after the introductory text had been written), Jones sent Frost his impressions and apologies: 'I like some of the reproductions & not others – the colour ones do strange things – in some cases... they get something of the feeling of the picture. But with my particular work... reproduction is the very devil of a job. I'm sorry that Ill-health & one thing & another got in the way of my giving advice, or suggestions to the printers at the time the [blocks] were being made, but in any case, I find the whole business & technique of reproduction very outside my province so that I doubt if any suggestions would have been helpful. It seems largely a matter of luck.'

Kenneth Clark was less good-natured in his assessment of the book: 'It is, alas, a complete failure,' he wrote to Frost. 'If, when the series was first started, I had known as much about colour as I do now I should have

39. Kathleen Raine, *The Land Unknown* (London: Hamish Hamilton, 1975), 128-9.

realised that it was quite impossible to do a book on every artist. I am afraid it will do him nothing but disservice.'

All was not lost. The reproductions may not have conveyed Jones' subtle genius, but Robin Ironside's introduction to the monograph remains one of the most useful biographical accounts of the artist to date. It continues to be heavily quoted in portraits of the artist and studies of his work; and indeed, John Rothenstein's chapter on Jones in volume two of *Modern English Painters*, owes a great deal to Ironside's pioneering text.

Another book marred by the war and Frost's sojourn in America was that on the artist Edward Bawden, who spent much of the war stationed in the Middle East. In this case however, the book suffered not from the artist's lack of commitment to the monograph but from his overzealous meddling and his boundless eagerness to get it to press.

Almost upon first receiving the text, composed by the architectural historian J.M. Richards in 1942, Bawden started fiddling with passages, and re-framing the figure, namely himself, that Richards had so carefully painted. In September 1944, he had sent Frost a long list of amendments, despite the fact that 'I think Jim has done very well, extremely well taking into consideration the subject: I shall congratulate him upon the creation of a very lively little creature whose antics have greatly amused me'. A month later there were more revisions. 'Really very little requires attention,' he wrote to Frost, 'except for the paragraph about my first impressions of Italy & I believe it would be easier for me to try to re-write this particular bit, giving a different twist to the sense though retaining as many of Jim's sentences as I can, rather than bother K.C. by asking him to undertake this ridiculously small job.

As Richards left for war duties in Cairo soon after submitting the introduction, he saw few of the alterations. The introduction had been written in Bawden's absence using information provided by the artist's wife, so Bawden saw his own adjustments merely as corrective measures, not in need of the author's consent. In October 1945, Bawden made final revisions, advising the unsuspecting Glover that: 'The text need not be submitted again to Mr Richards (who is in Cairo) as that is unnecessary and would waste time.' Glover thus sent the proofs to press without passing them through Richards' hands.

Bawden's interest in the volume was by no means confined to its text. In his exquisite minuscule handwriting (a habit formed while he was engaged doing small comic drawings for a weekly comic strip for the Middle East picture paper, *Parade*) he also composed meticulous instructions to Glover regarding the illustrations. These came replete with small sketches. Fortunately, most of his work had already been photographed officially at the MoI, so the problem of collecting together pictures was circumvented. But there was still the question of the portrait of himself. The photograph he had sent Frost of himself and Antony Gross against a painted background of palms and pyramids, had gone missing in the confusion at Harmondsworth. After seeing the pulls, Bawden remarked woefully, and with characteristic vanity:

I am rather disappointed, as I would have preferred the one of myself seated against a painted background of palms & pyramids, which was taken in Cairo. It is a trifle fantastic, more in keeping with my nature; also it makes me look less middle-aged than I am. This compulsory photograph was taken by the BBC, in an exceptionally bare, cold, underground chamber. The photographer pulled out my tie & pushed a fountain pen in my hand – he arranged me like a vase of flowers, & was indifferent to the fact that my tie is generally crooked & I never use one of the wretched fountain pens.

When Bawden's volume finally arrived late in 1947, it was the author, Richards', turn to be distressed: 'The text, incidentally, contains one unaccountable alteration of my script which makes nonsense of one sentence as well as a couple of misprints,' he wrote to Frost, 'but I wouldn't think of complaining about these as I have done enough complaining to you already and anyway they are nothing in relation to the achievement of getting the book out and in such an elegant form.' Richards indirectly incriminated Frost, but it turned out that the problems were due to Bawden's endless meddling:

I have just been speaking to Edward and find that the alteration in my text that I mentioned to you was made not by you but by him – when you got him to correct a proof during my absence abroad... It naturally struck me as not only different from what I had written, but a nonsensical thing to say anyway. But I was too hasty in blaming you for it. And what is worse, on re-reading the text I found the other misprint I thought I had spotted wasn't one after all, which makes me feel very bad – like the worst kind of fault-finding author of which you must have too much experience. The only thing I can do is to apologise humbly. Your record of accuracy remains unblemished; it is mine that now becomes tarnished.

Reluctantly, Frost let the blame fall elsewhere: 'I must say – although it is perhaps unbecoming to do so – that the final putting together was not done by me, but handled here by someone else whilst I was in America.'

In 1948, *Ben Nicholson, William Nicholson* and *Frances Hodgkins,* appeared in two batches, followed by *David Jones* the following August. They garnered less attention in the press than earlier volumes. There were competitors now: additions to The Faber Gallery, such as *Matisse* and *Chagall*, that inspired two-column reviews in journals like the *New English Weekly,* and *The Observer.*

The Penguin volumes may have gone largely unnoticed in the press, but they were welcomed with open arms by the authors and artists who had long awaited them – at least, those individuals that were still alive. Since 1947, William Nicholson had been living in a nursing home in Roehampton specialising in depression, where he had been placed by Marguerite Steen. His painting days were over, and he suffered from memory loss, 'black moods' and 'small destructive ways'.[40] When his son Ben visited him in November

1947, the younger artist found him 'half withdrawn from existence' and almost in another world. Previous to his admittance, his health, both mental and physical, had been failing. At one point, he had persuaded Churchill to return a painting he had made of Winston and Clementine, 'ostensibly so that he could do further work on it'. When the painting arrived, he fell into a fit of despair, decided that the work was sub-standard, and threw it into the fire.

The 1948 arrival of the Penguin monograph, in contrast, was one of the most uplifting events at the end of Nicholson's life. It made little impact on his reputation, but it raised his spirits. 'It was a great pleasure to receive the William Nicholson Penguins at last, and in time for Christmas,' Steen said to Frost: 'Sir William spent a very happy morning looking at them, and, I think, was very pleased with the general presentation of his work.' William Nicholson's biographer, Sarah Jane Checkland, noted: 'His only pleasure was in looking at the Penguin monograph on him when it was published in 1948.' Sadly, his friend Robert Nichols, who had written the introduction years earlier was denied this pleasure. As Kenneth Clark wrote to Frost: 'What a long time it seems since we first planned [these volumes]. Bob Nichols must have been dead for three years. I realise that this is not your fault, but it is not much encouragement to authorship.'

The elderly Frances Hodgkins, who had waited so patiently, so long, likewise missed seeing Penguin volumes of her work on display in the local bookshops in St Ives. A year before her monograph was published, she died in a mental hospital near Dorchester. During the rare lucid moments at the end of her life, she urged her friends to remember her as she had been, not as she was. Her death was announced on the BBC and obituaries appeared in *The Times*, *Art News*, *Manchester Guardian* and *The Burlington Magazine*. Though she missed out on the long awaited volume, her life did not end in disappointment. A few months before she died, a Retrospective Exhibition of her work at the Lefevre Gallery was covered widely by the popular press, where she was lauded as the 'Grand Old Lady' of British painting, and 'one of the master colourists of our time'. When the Penguin monograph appeared, it was received with praise and open hearts. Ben Nicholson informed Frost with sober respect: 'I still think [Frances Hodgkins] is one of the most successful in the series.'

Ben Nicholson cheerfully welcomed his monograph several months before his father's appeared, though William Nicholson is listed before him as MP12. It came at an auspicious time in his life. The doldrums of the war were over, his reputation was on an upswing, and the years of watching the sky and sea of Cornwall had brought to his work a new refreshing dimension. The monograph was accompanied by the first of two folio volumes on his work published by Lund Humphries. Rather than vying for attention, the books complemented each other. John Summerson's exegesis

40. Checkland, 252.

of his work in the Penguin series as a 'continuous journey from point to point – a journey of metaphysical goals', remained 'the basis for all Ben Nicholson studies'.[41] Ben liked to call the book his 'Odyssey'.[42] The Lund Humphries tome, in contrast, was a major luxurious production, but it was less likely to reach the broad audience the Penguin volume promised, and Herbert Read's introduction was more a tract on abstract art than a discussion of Ben Nicholson's life and oeuvre. After years of hardship, Ben Nicholson finally knew he had landed on safe ground when Sir Kenneth Clark, the man who had only reluctantly admitted him into the Penguin series in the first place, purchased two of his works for £40 and £80.[43]

The success of the early *Penguin Modern Painters* encouraged Penguin to plan a series of *Penguin Prints*, which also appeared for the first time in 1948 under the editorship of Bernhard Baer. In some ways the plan made a great deal of economic sense. A monograph with thirty-two plates, sixteen in colour, was an organisational labyrinth, and when sold – by now – for three shillings and sixpence amounted to a small net gain for the company. A single plate, lovingly produced in seven, eight, or nine colours, and mounted in a folder could be sold for a good six shillings, and even with the practice amongst art world retailers of taking 50 per cent profit from the cover price, this translated into tidy profits. The first prints were of paintings by J.M.W. Turner, Paul Klee, John Piper, and Pablo Picasso. These were followed by another Paul Klee, and works by Amadeo Modigliani, Henry Moore, Pieter de Hooch, Samuel Palmer and Paul Cézanne. A review in *The New Statesman and Nation*, written not long before Christmas by Robert Melville, one of the best critics of the day, provided good publicity:

> One good colour plate is worth any number of bad ones, and it must be said that the new Penguin prints meet the demand for colour reproductions in a much more admirable fashion than the comparable books. Each of the four beautifully printed reproductions so far published is in a protective folder which at a pinch would serve as a mount... if I back the Picasso to sell out a little ahead of the others in spite of its being in black and white it is because it looks so astonishingly like the original aquatint.

Despite all good intentions, marketing was the demise of the *Penguin Print* initiative. An excerpt from *The Penguin Story* explains:

> This venture had limited success, not certainly through any lack of merit but simply because of marketing difficulties. Print shops are few and far between and therefore provided only a modest outlet for the sale of Penguin Prints. Bookshops and bookstalls, on the other hand, have very limited facilities for the display of prints, and this estimable endeavour failed to reach the notice of the buying public on a wide enough scale.

41. Norbert Lynton, *Ben Nicholson* (London: Phaidon, 1993), 221.
42. Checkland, 251.
43. Checkland, 251.

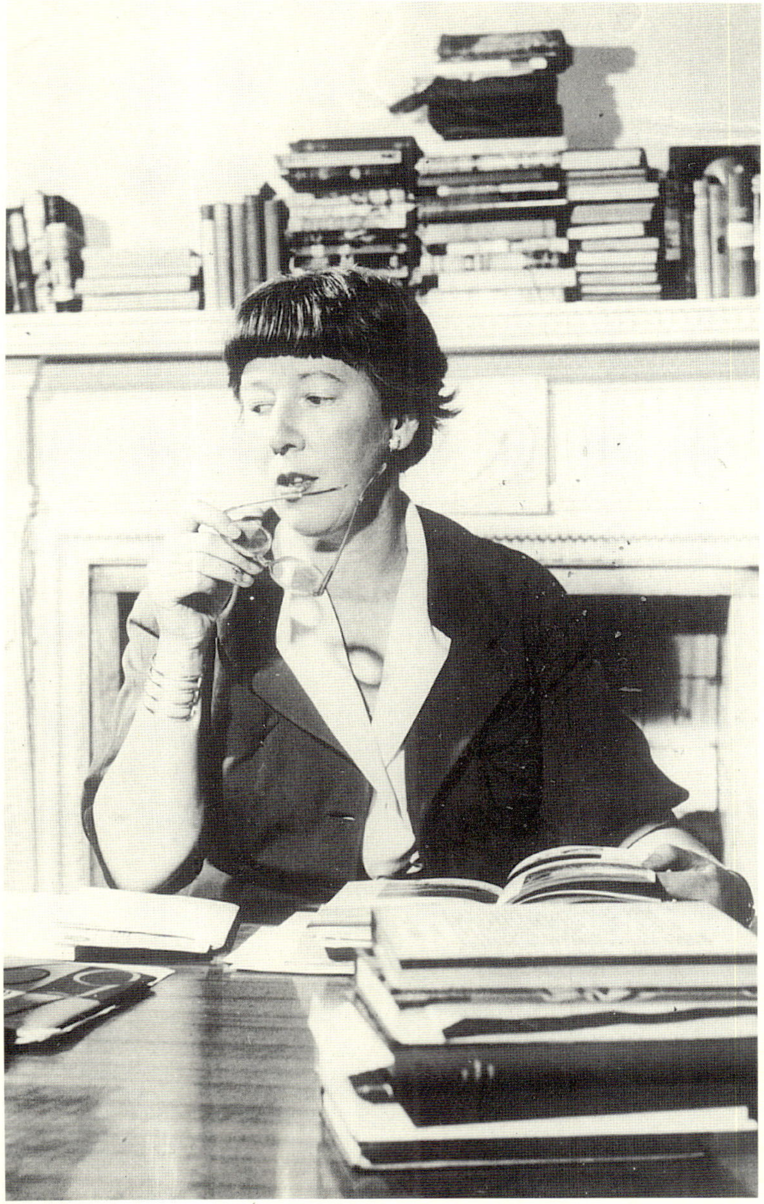

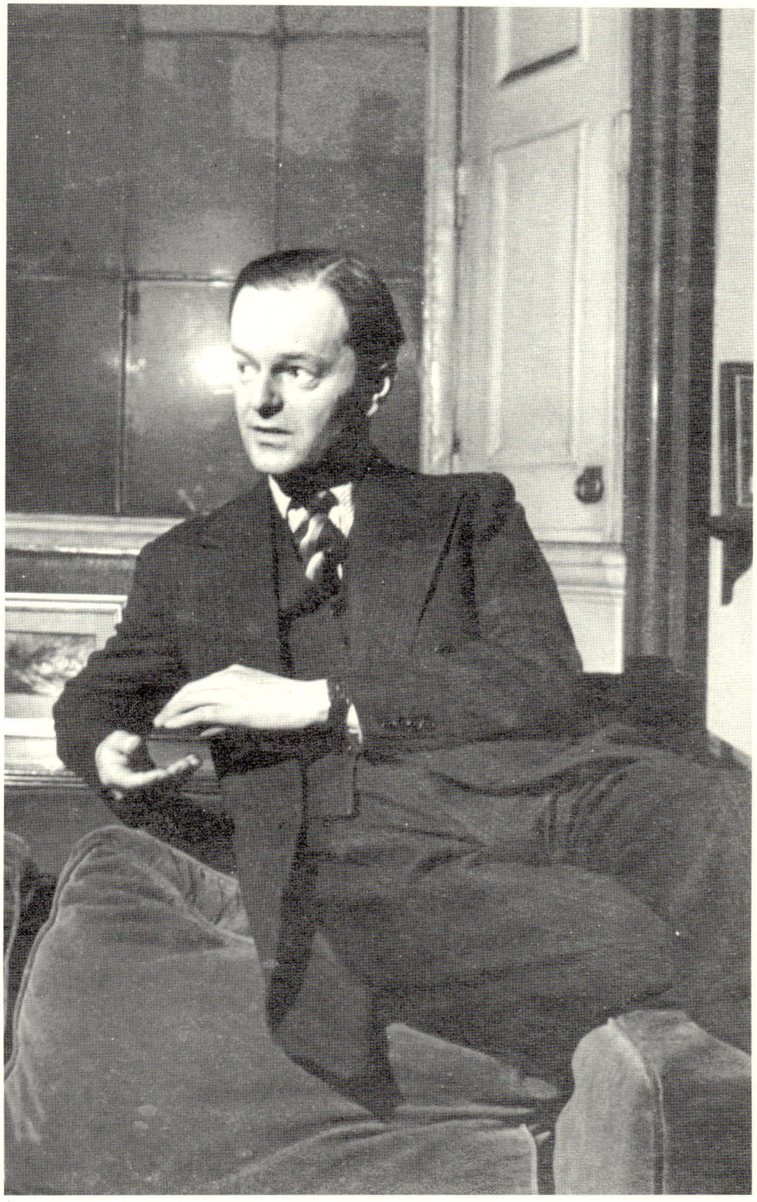

Eunice Frost and Sir Kenneth Clark

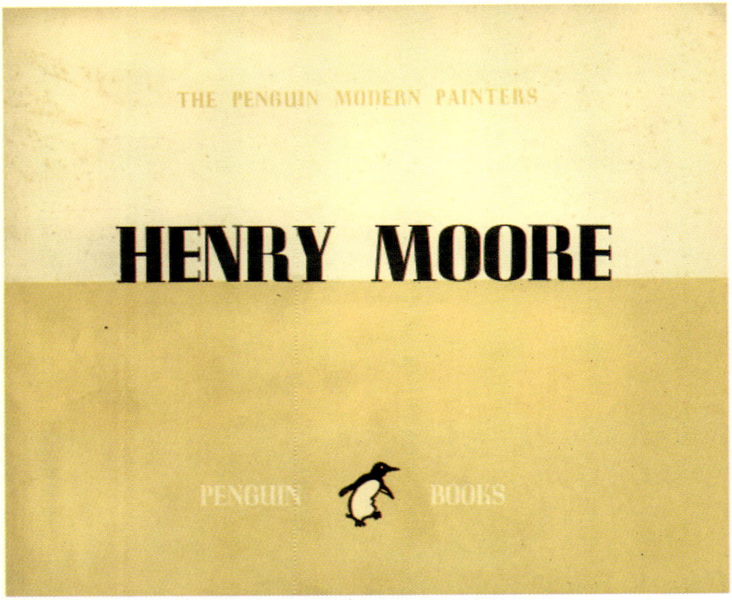
THE PENGUIN MODERN PAINTERS
HENRY MOORE
PENGUIN
BOOKS

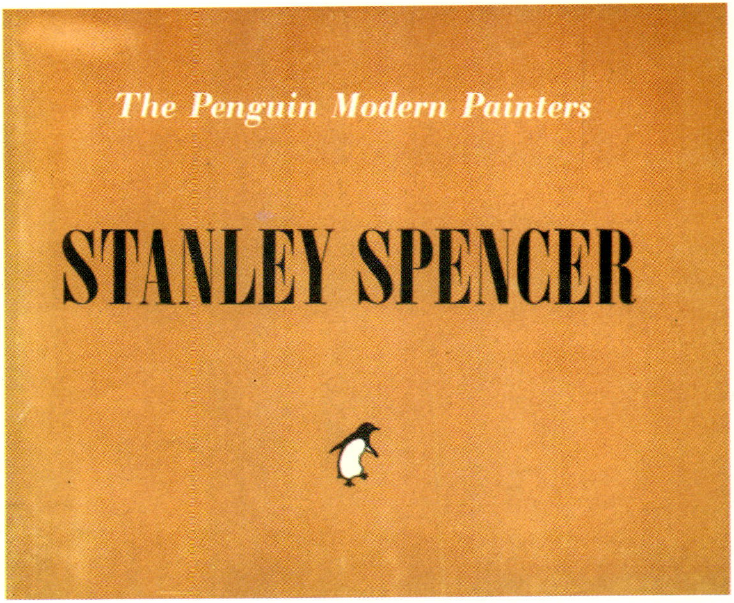
The Penguin Modern Painters
STANLEY SPENCER

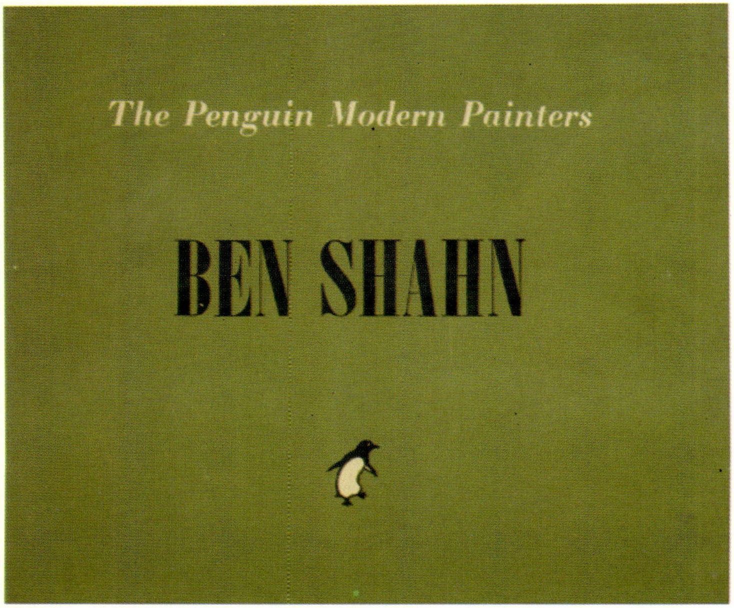
The Penguin Modern Painters
BEN SHAHN

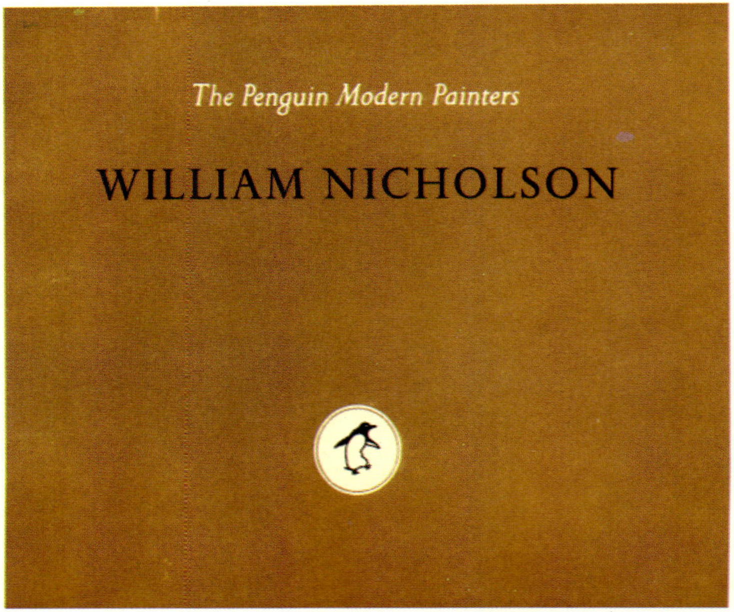
The Penguin Modern Painters
WILLIAM NICHOLSON

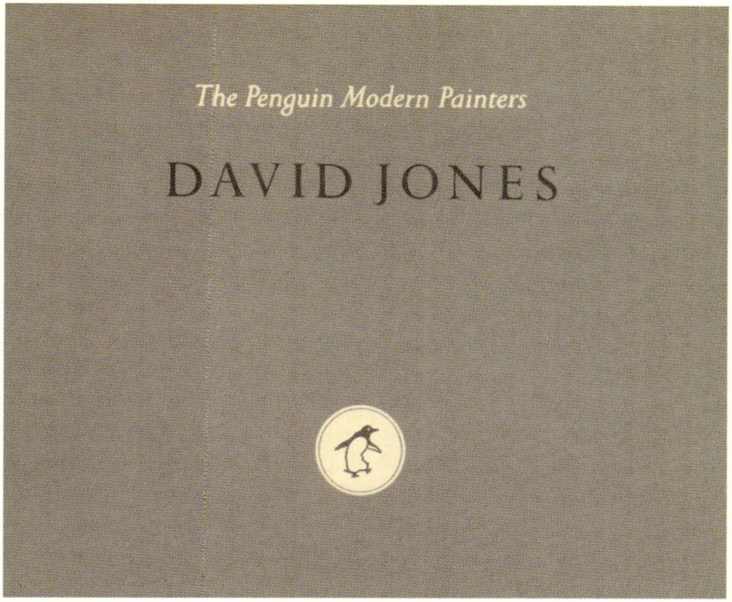

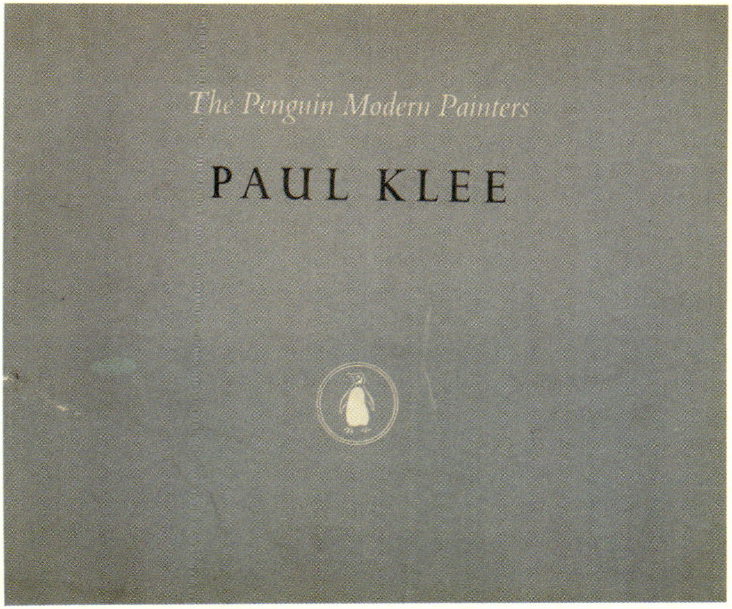

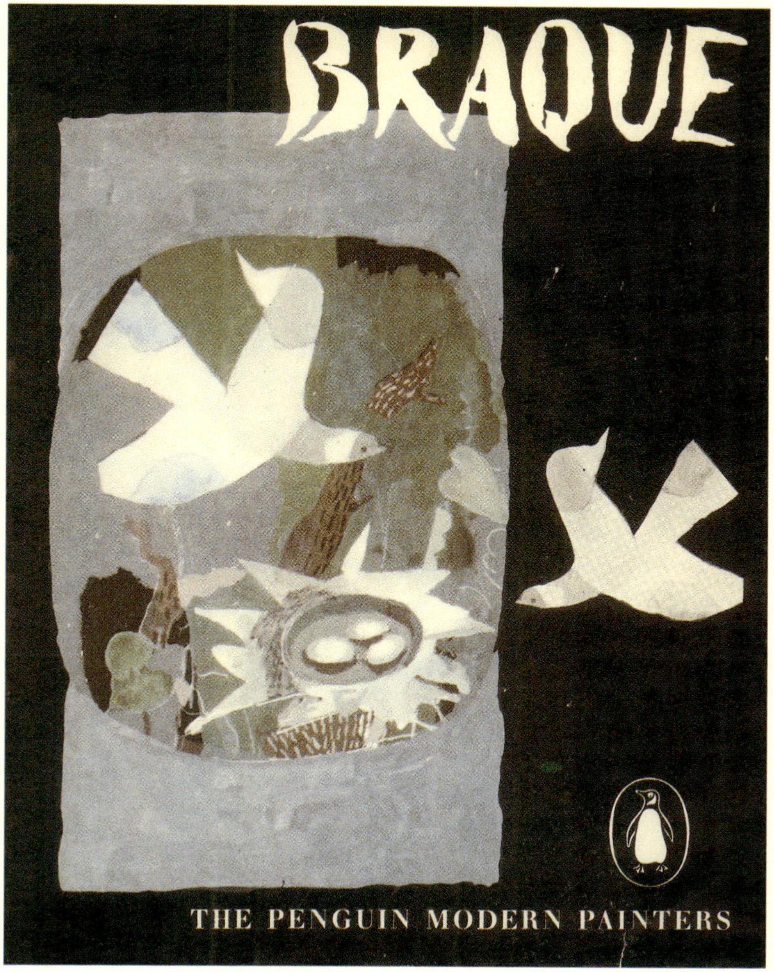

Cover styles

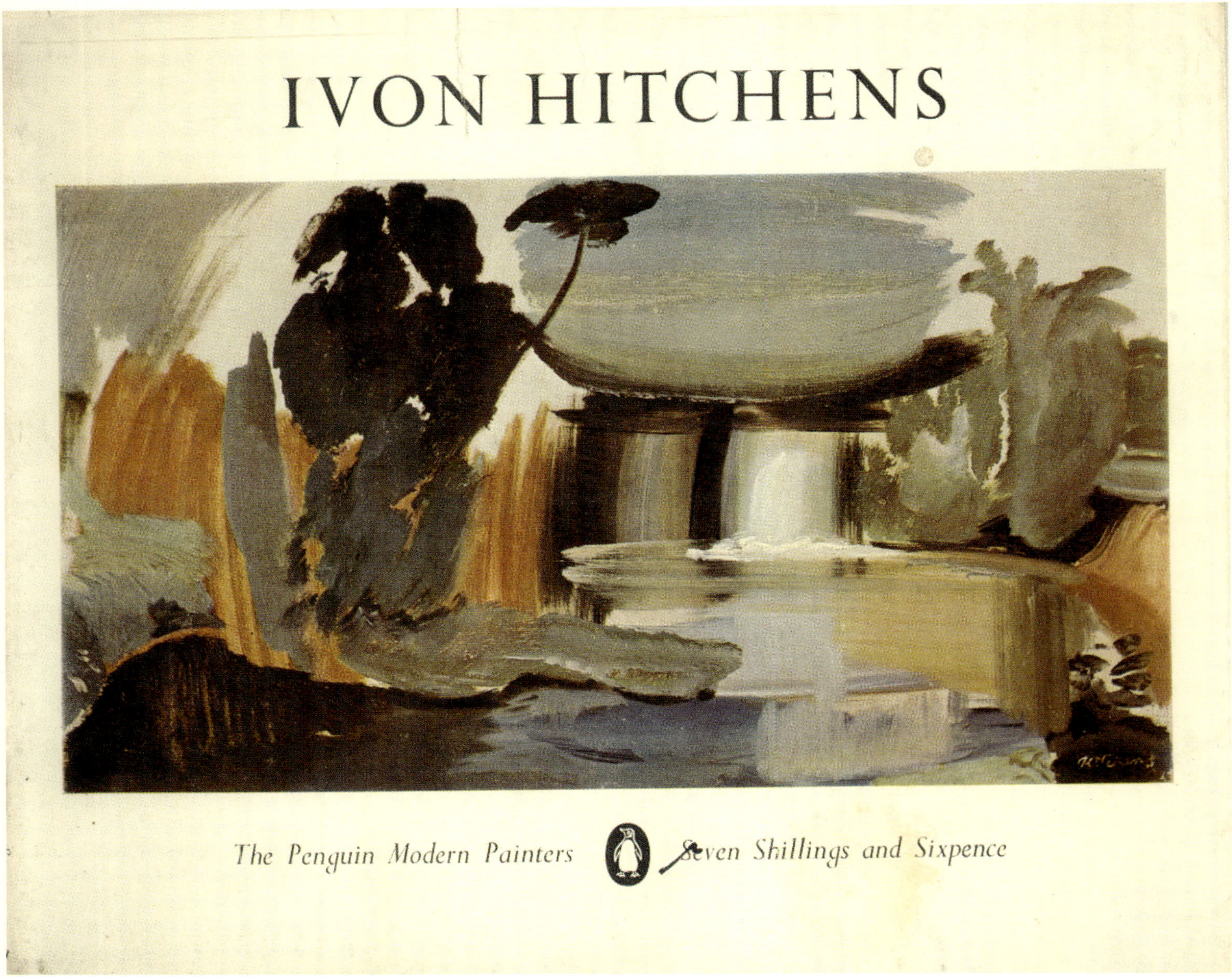

Ivon Hitchens dust wrapper

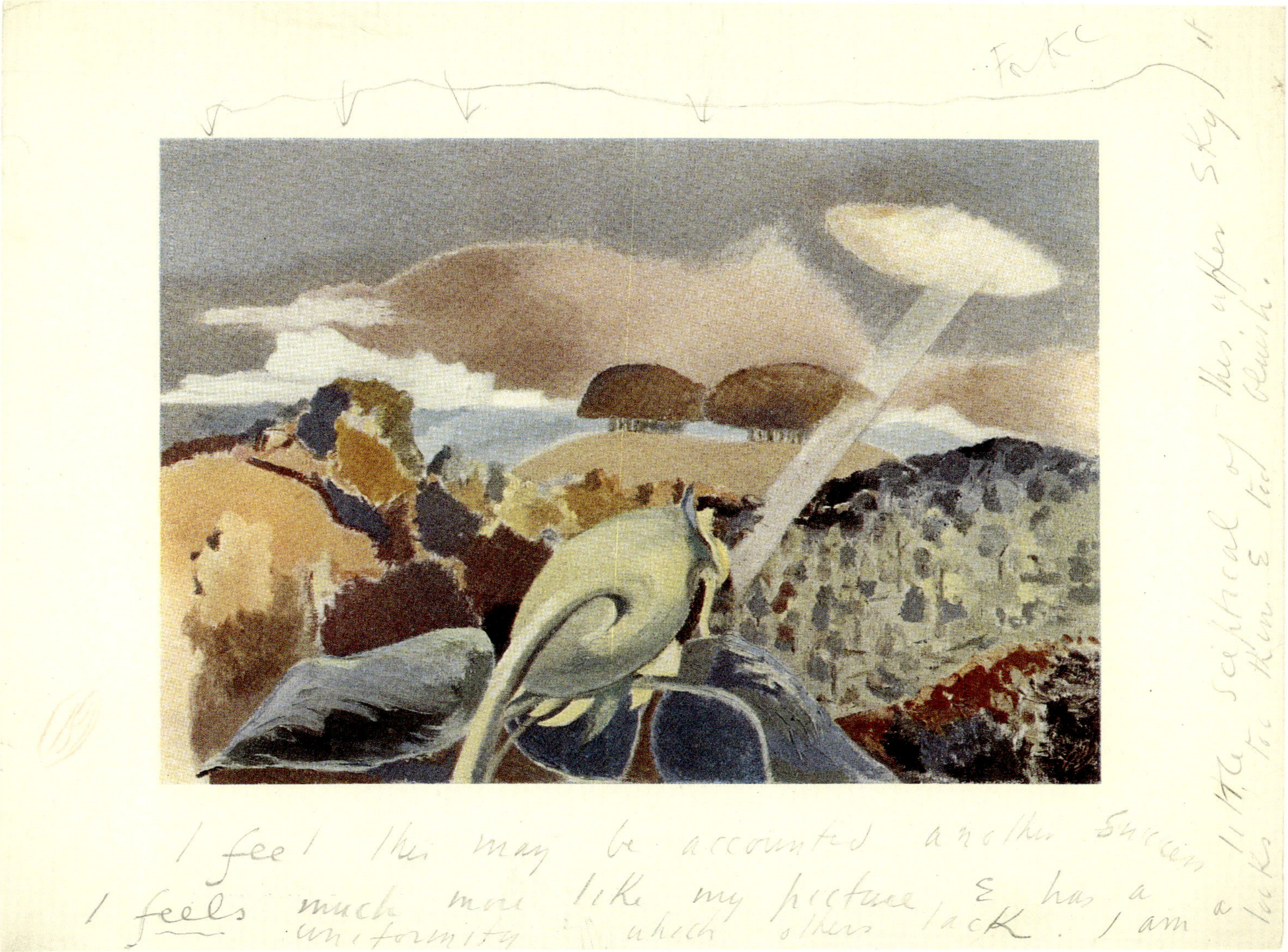

Paul Nash proof sheet and hand-written comments

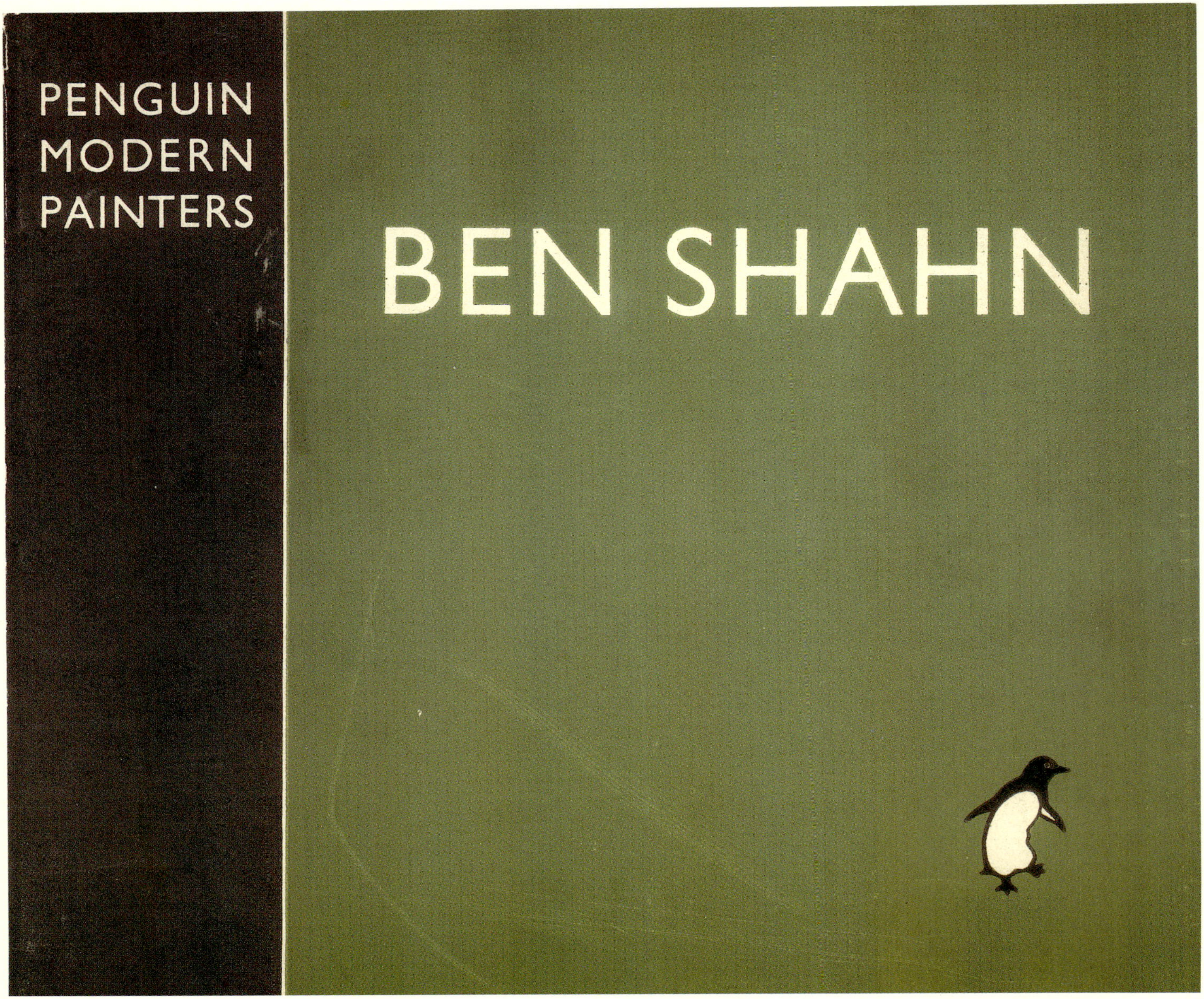

Ben Shahn: MoMA New York edition front cover

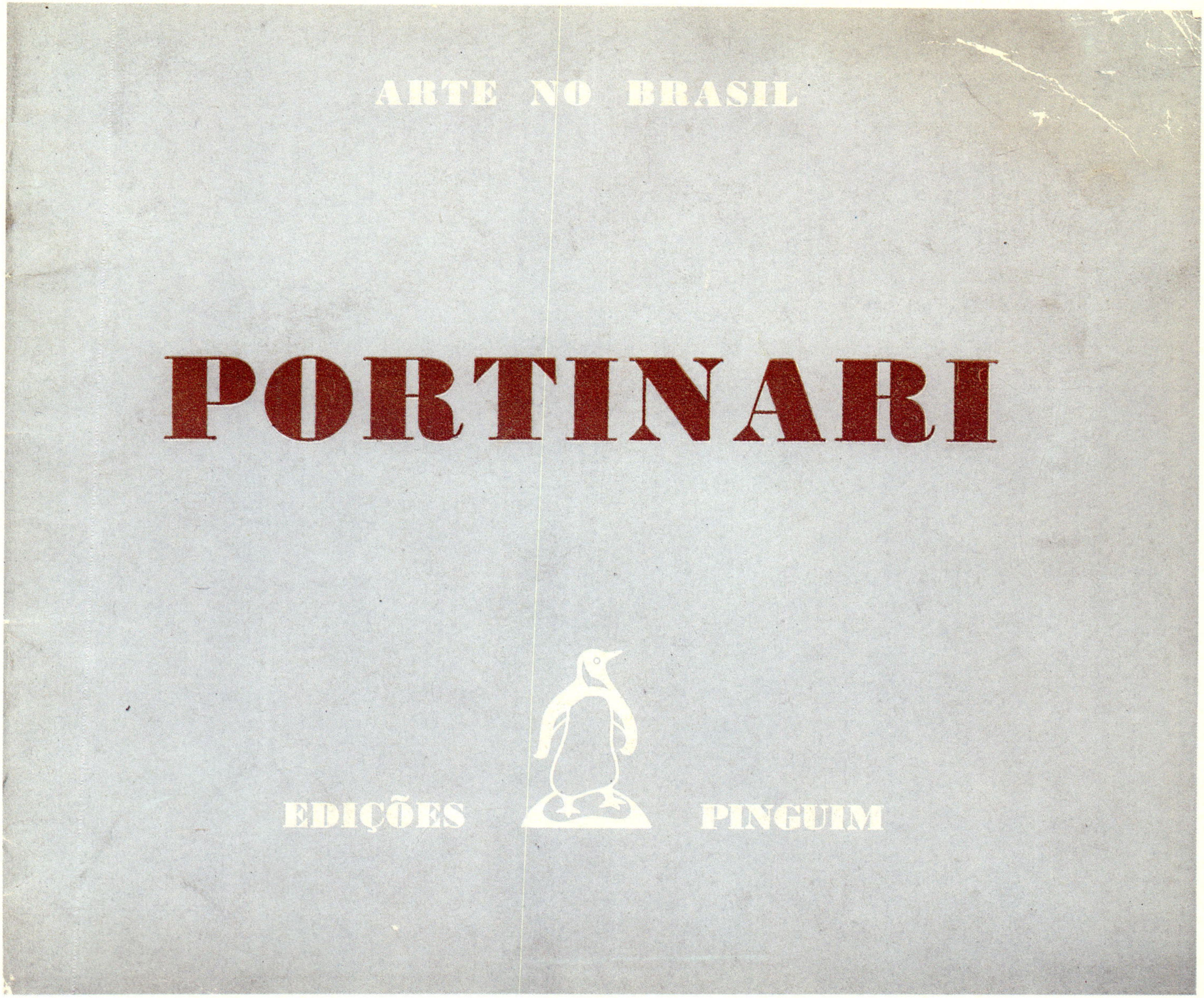

Portinari front cover

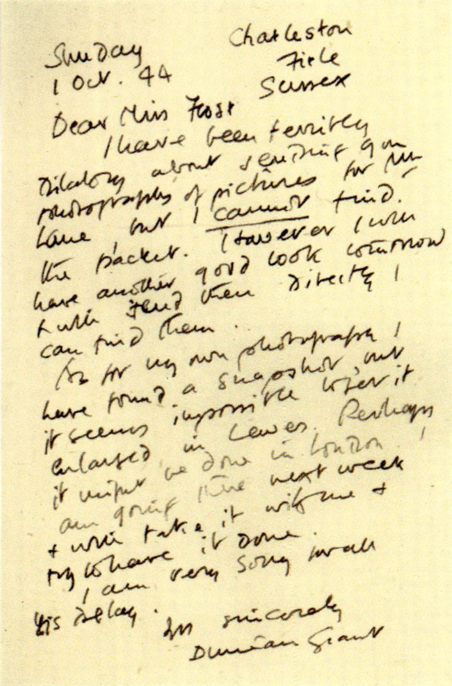

Sunday
1 Oct. 44

Charleston
Firle
Sussex

Dear Miss Frost
I have been terribly dilatory about sending you photographs of pictures for the Lane but I cannot find the packet. However I will have another good look tomorrow & will send them directly I can find them.

As for my own photograph I have found a snapshot, but it seems impossible to get it enlarged in Lewes. Perhaps it might be done in London. I am going there next week & will take it with me & try to have it done.

I am very sorry for all this delay.

Yrs sincerely
Duncan Grant

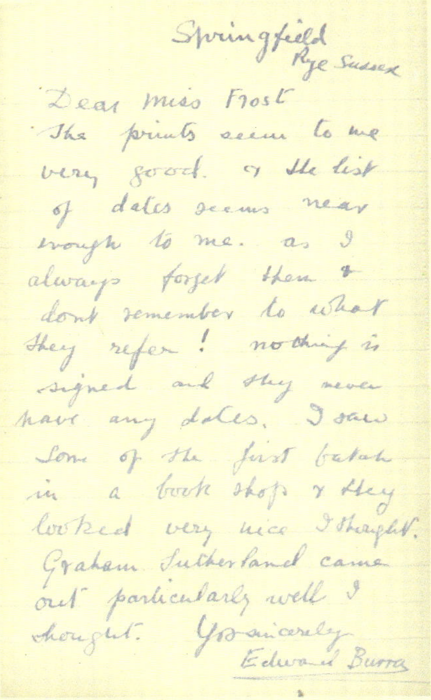

Springfield
Rye Sussex

Dear Miss Frost
The prints seem to me very good. & the list of dates seems near enough to me. as I always forget them & dont remember to what they refer! nothing is signed and they never have any dates. I saw some of the first batch in a book shop & they looked very nice I thought. Graham Sutherland came out particularly well I thought.

Yrs sincerely
Edward Burra

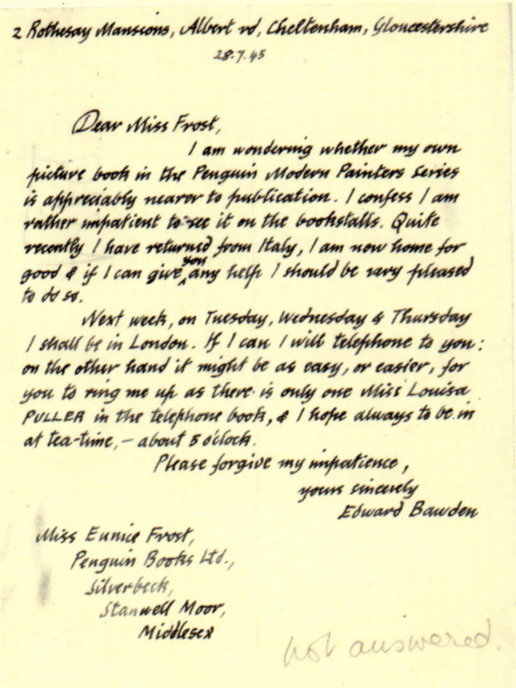

2 Rothesay Mansions, Albert rd, Cheltenham, Gloucestershire
28.7.45

Dear Miss Frost,

I am wondering whether my own picture book in the Penguin Modern Painters Series is appreciably nearer to publication. I confess I am rather impatient to see it on the bookstalls. Quite recently I have returned from Italy, I am now home for good & if I can give you any help I should be very pleased to do so.

Next week, on Tuesday, Wednesday & Thursday I shall be in London. If I can I will telephone to you: on the other hand it might be as easy, or easier, for you to ring me up as there is only one Miss Louisa PULLER in the telephone book, & I hope always to be in at tea-time, – about 5 o'clock.

Please forgive my impatience,

yours sincerely
Edward Bawden

Miss Eunice Frost,
Penguin Books Ltd.,
Silverbeck,
Stanwell Moor,
Middlesex

Not answered.

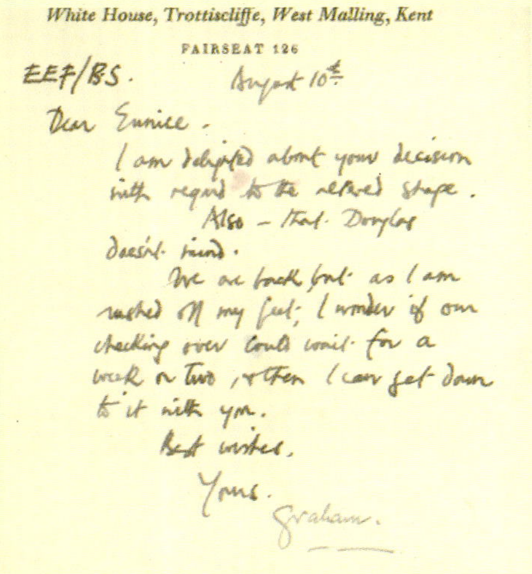

White House, Trottiscliffe, West Malling, Kent

FAIRSEAT 126

EEF/BS. August 10th.

Dear Eunice.
I am delighted about your decision with regard to the altered shape.
Also – that Douglas doesn't mind.
We are back but as I am rushed off my feet; I wonder if our checking over could wait for a week or two, & then I can get down to it with you.
Best wishes.
Yours.
Graham.

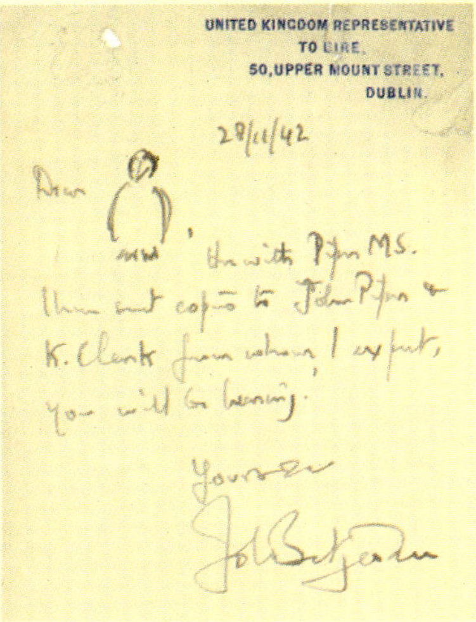

UNITED KINGDOM REPRESENTATIVE
TO EIRE.
50, UPPER MOUNT STREET,
DUBLIN.

28/11/42

Dear [drawing],

Herewith Piper MS.
I have sent copies to John Piper & K. Clark from whom, I expect, you will be hearing.

Yours ever
John Betjeman

Selected correspondence

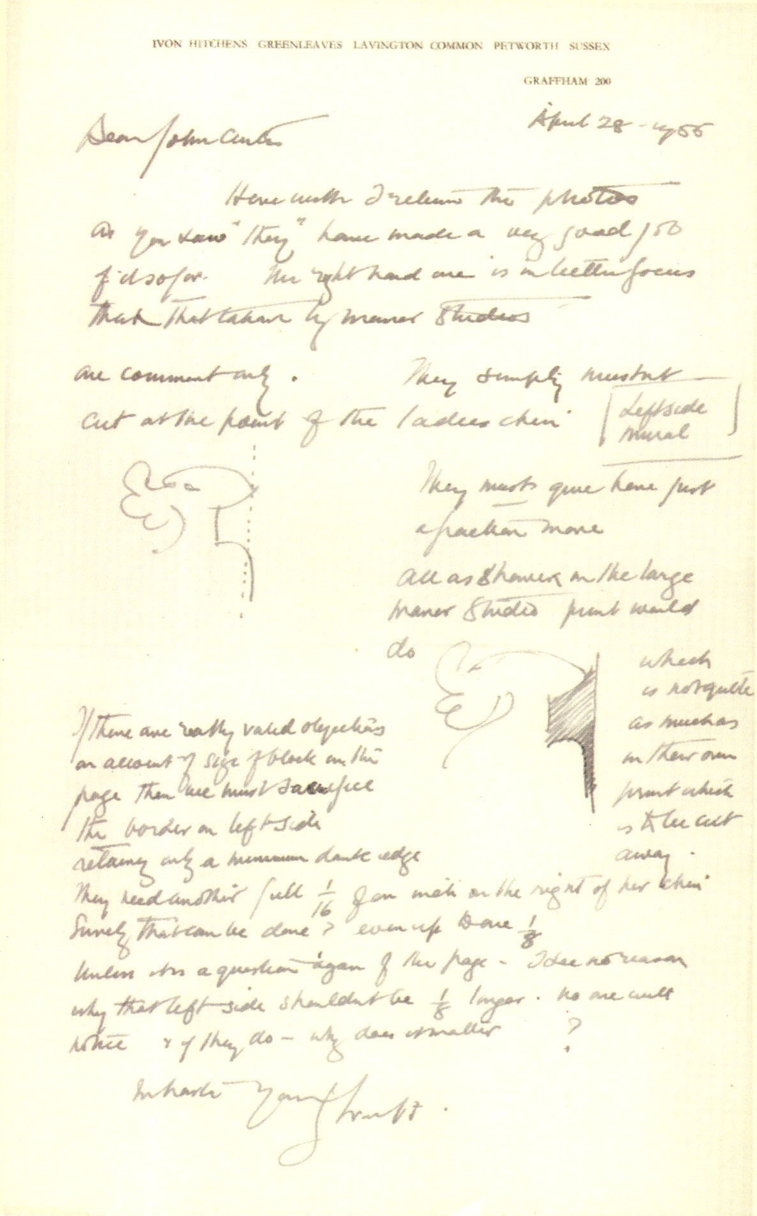

IVON HITCHENS GREENLEAVES LAVINGTON COMMON PETWORTH SUSSEX

GRAFFHAM 200

April 28 – 1956

Dear John Carter

Herewith I return the photos
As you saw "they" have made a very good job
of it so far. The right hand one is in better focus
than that taken by Manor Studios

one comment only. They simply mustn't
cut at the point of the ladies chin [Left side mural]

They must give here just
a fraction more
all as shown on the large
Manor Studio print would
do
which is not quite as much as in their own print which is to be cut away.

If there are really valid objections
on account of size of block on the
page then we must sacrifice
the border on left side
retaining only a minimum dark edge
They need another full 1/16 of an inch on the right of her chin
Surely that can be done? even up to [illegible] 1/8
Unless it is a question again of the page – I see no reason
why that left side shouldn't be 1/8 longer. No one will
notice & if they do – why does it matter ?

In haste Yours [illegible]

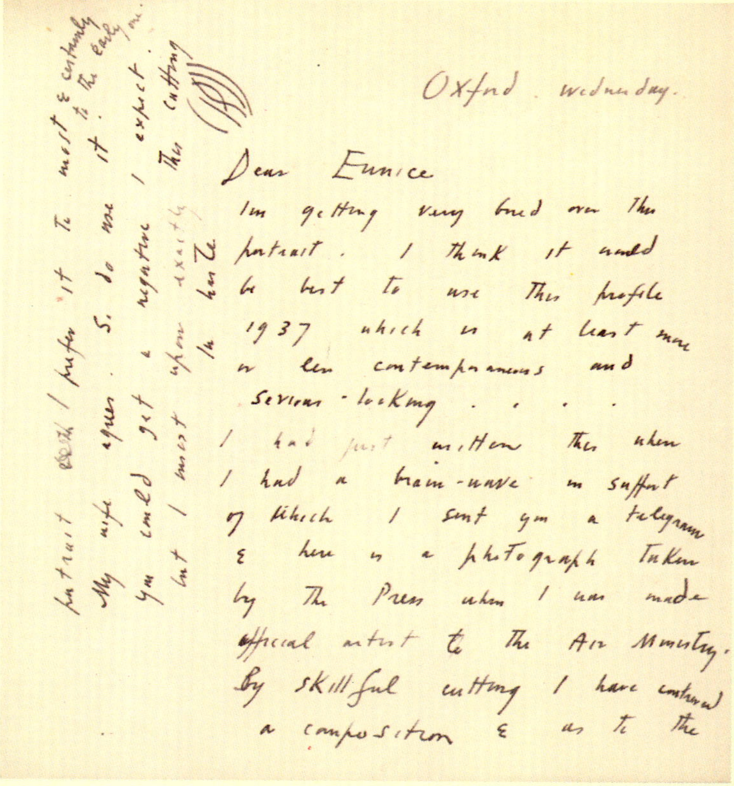

Oxford . Wednesday.

Dear Eunice
I'm getting very tired over this
portrait. I think it would
be best to use this profile
1937 which is at least more
or less contemporaneous and
serious-looking . . .
I had just written this when
I had a brain-wave in support
of which I sent you a telegram
& here is a photograph taken
by the Press when I was made
official artist to the Air Ministry.
By skillful cutting I have contrived
a composition & as to the

portrait ~~both~~ I prefer it to most & certainly to the early one.
My wife agrees. So do use it.
You could get a negative I expect
but I must [insist] upon exactly this cutting
In haste

Selected correspondence

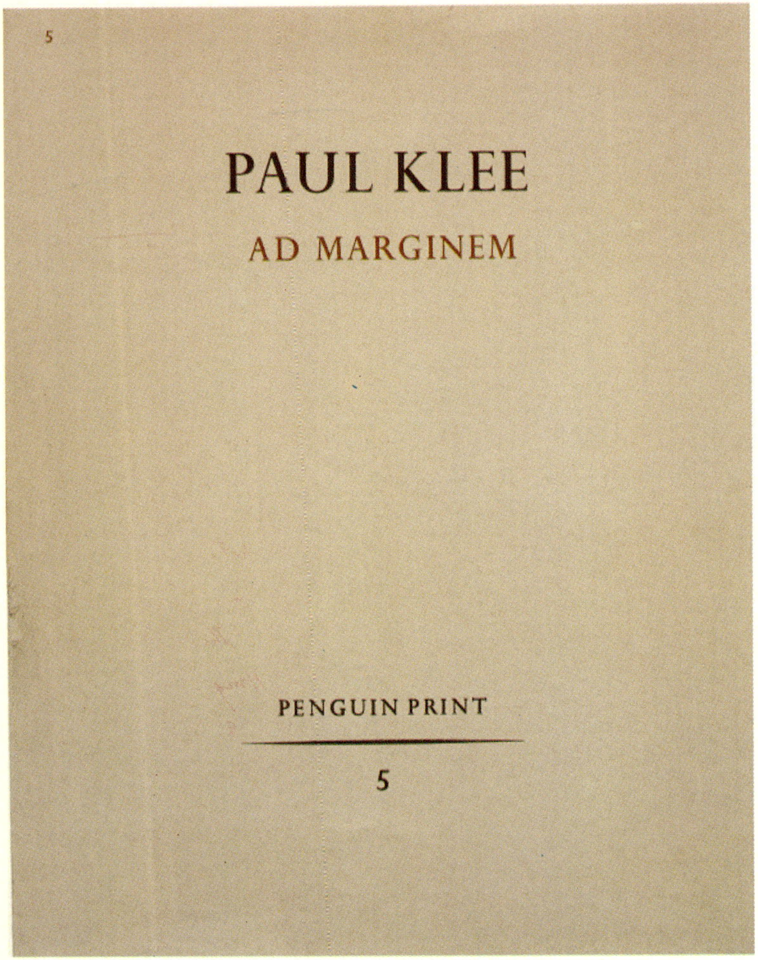

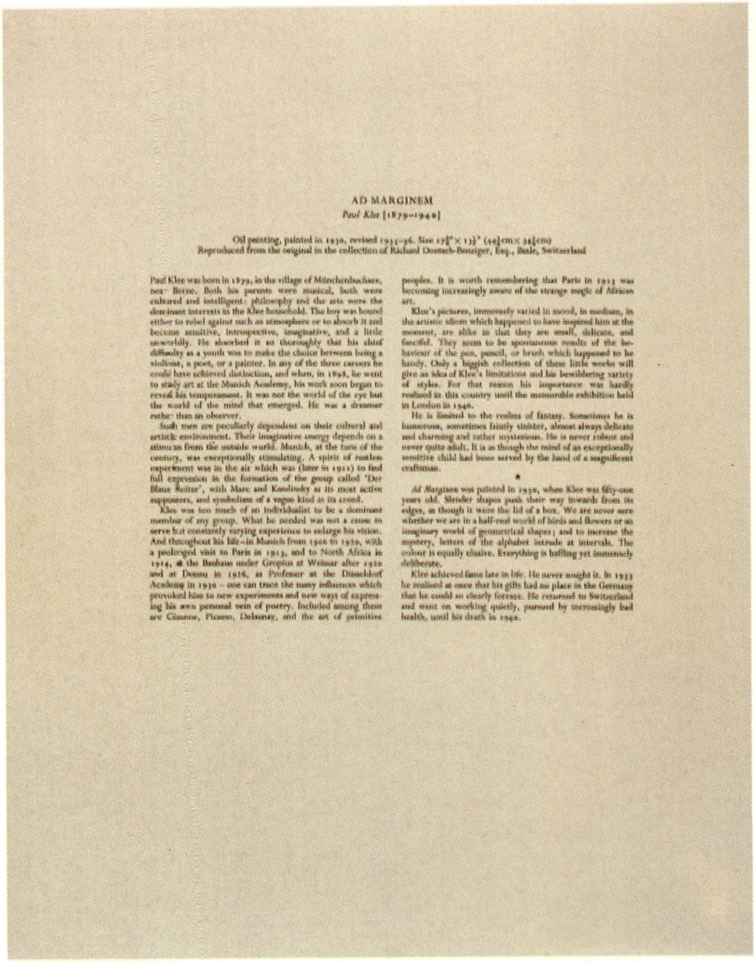

AD MARGINEM

Paul Klee [1879–1940]

Oil painting, painted in 1930, revised 1935–36. Size 17⅞" × 13½" (45⅜cm × 34⅜cm)
Reproduced from the original in the collection of Richard Doetsch-Benziger, Esq., Basle, Switzerland

Paul Klee was born in 1879, in the village of Münchenbuchsee, near Berne. Both his parents were musical, both were cultured and intelligent: philosophy and the arts were the dominant interests in the Klee household. The boy was bound either to rebel against such an atmosphere or to absorb it and become sensitive, introspective, imaginative, and a little unworldly. He absorbed it so thoroughly that his chief difficulty as a youth was to make the choice between being a violinist, a poet, or a painter. In any of the three careers he could have achieved distinction, and when, in 1898, he went to study art at the Munich Academy, his work soon began to reveal his temperament. It was not the world of the eye but the world of the mind that emerged. He was a dreamer rather than an observer.

Such men are peculiarly dependent on their cultural and artistic environment. Their imaginative energy depends on a stimulus from the outside world. Munich, at the turn of the century, was exceptionally stimulating. A spirit of restless experiment was in the air which was (later in 1911) to find full expression in the formation of the group called 'Der Blaue Reiter', with Marc and Kandinsky as its most active supporters, and symbolism of a vague kind as its creed.

Klee was too much of an individualist to be a dominant member of any group. What he needed was not a cause to serve but constantly varying experience to enlarge his vision. And throughout his life – in Munich from 1906 to 1920, with a prolonged visit to Paris in 1913, and to North Africa in 1914, at the Bauhaus under Gropius at Weimar after 1920 and at Dessau in 1926, as Professor at the Düsseldorf Academy in 1930 – one can trace the many influences which provoked him to new experiments and new ways of expressing his own personal vein of poetry. Included among them are Cézanne, Picasso, Delaunay, and the art of primitive peoples. It is worth remembering that Paris in 1913 was becoming increasingly aware of the strange magic of African art.

Klee's pictures, immensely varied in mood, in medium, in the artistic idiom which happened to have inspired him at the moment, are alike in that they are small, delicate, and fanciful. They seem to be spontaneous results of the behaviour of the pen, pencil, or brush which happened to be handy. Only a biggish collection of these little works will give an idea of Klee's limitations and his bewildering variety of styles. For that reason his importance was hardly realised in this country until the memorable exhibition held in London in 1946.

He is limited to the realms of fantasy. Sometimes he is humorous, sometimes faintly sinister, almost always delicate and charming and rather mysterious. He is never robust and never quite adult. It is as though the mind of an exceptionally sensitive child had been served by the hand of a magnificent craftsman.

*

Ad Marginem was painted in 1930, when Klee was fifty-one years old. Slender shapes push their way inwards from its edges, as though it were the lid of a box. We are never sure whether we are in a half-real world of birds and flowers or an imaginary world of geometrical shapes; and to increase the mystery, letters of the alphabet intrude at intervals. The colour is equally elusive. Everything is baffling yet immensely deliberate.

Klee achieved fame late in life. He never sought it. In 1933 he realised at once that his gifts had no place in the Germany that he could so clearly foresee. He returned to Switzerland and went on working quietly, pursued by increasingly bad health, until his death in 1940.

Penguin Prints: folder front cover and inside front cover (actual size 430 x 340mm)

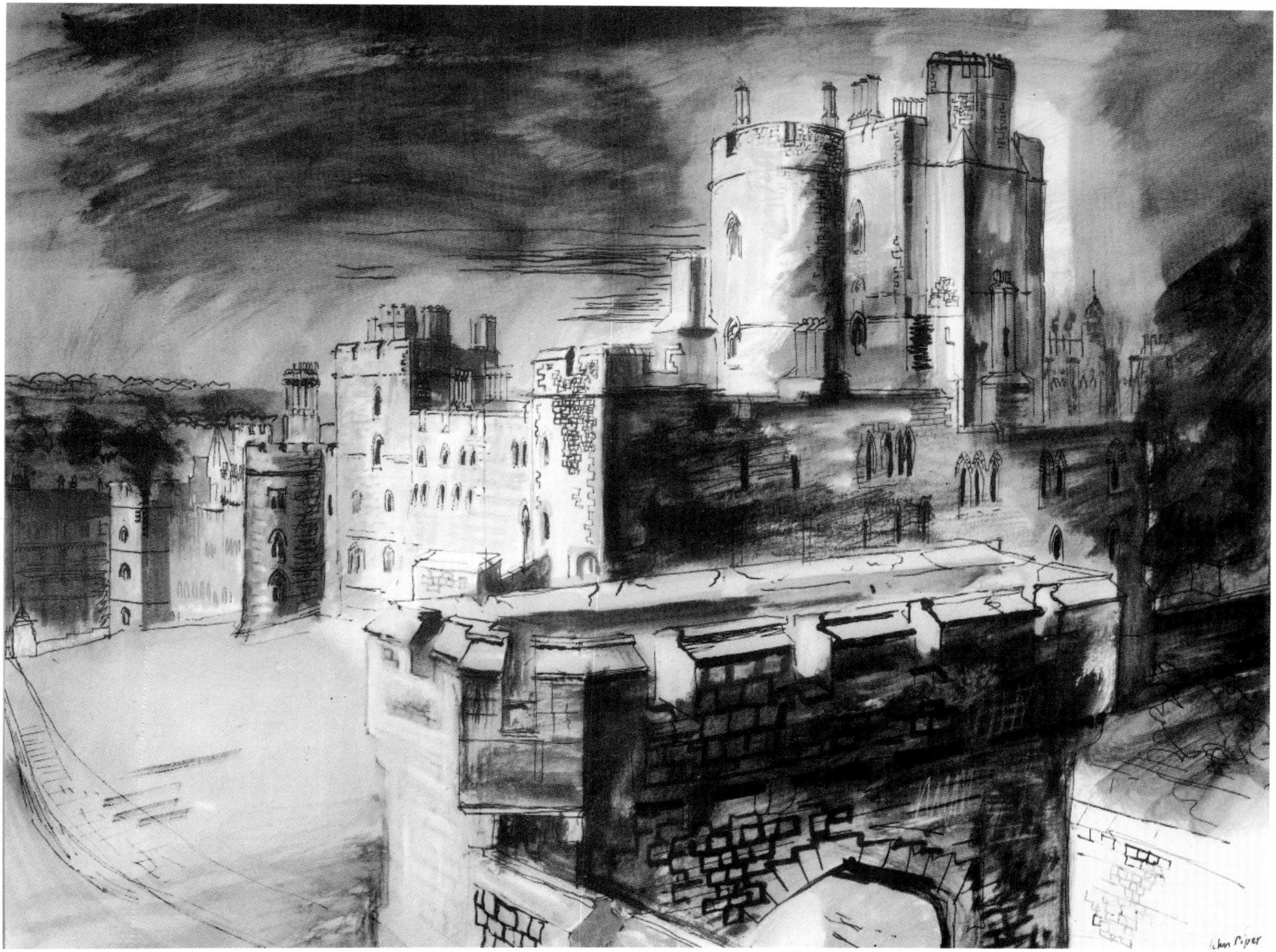

Penguin Print 3: John Piper, *View of Windsor Castle* (actual size 355 x 265mm)

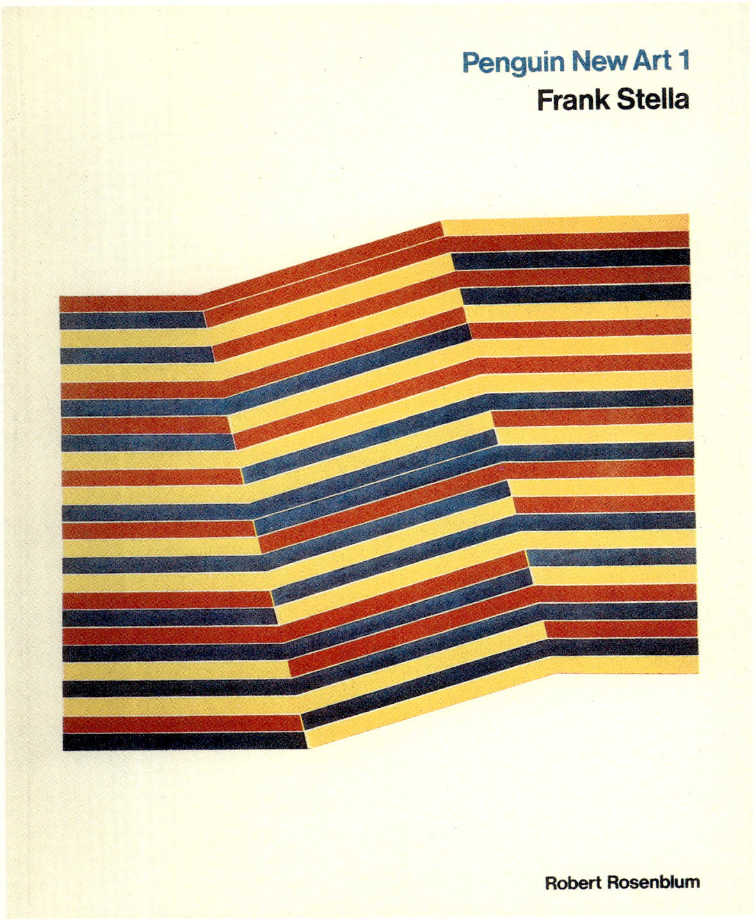

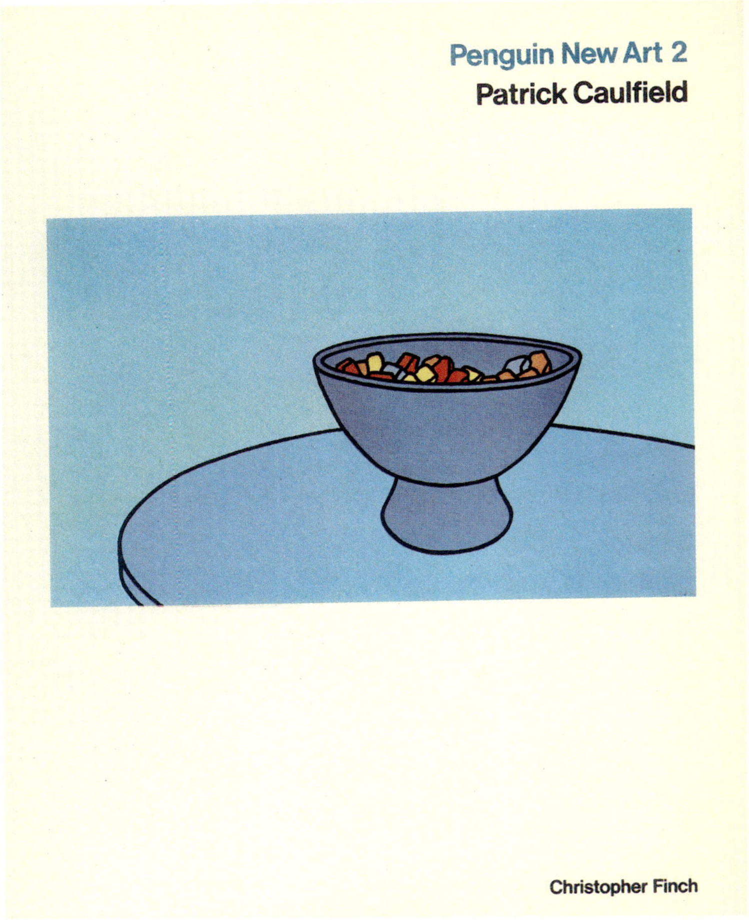

Penguin New Art 1 and 2 (actual size 99 x 120mm)

INTERNATIONAL

THOSE who knew Allen Lane tended to describe him as a man who would never let Penguin rest on its laurels. He was an expansionist and an ideas man and he was always putting new projects on the fire. It was up to people like Frost and Glover whether or not these projects simmered or boiled. Morpurgo, in *Master of None*, describes Harmondsworth after the war as 'a pirate ship', but its description could equally be applied to Lane himself:

> A privateer dashing but honourable, its objectives such treasures as could be found anywhere on oceans charted and uncharted, its ultimate intention the conquest of empire, imperial dominion over all the continents be they continents known to geography or the continents of imagination and scholarship.

Lane's drive to imperial dominion was no less true of *The Penguin Modern Painters* than of his company at large. With an office in the US and branches opening in South America and Australia, it made sense, Lane thought, to start up series of Modern Painters specific to these regions. It also seemed a good idea to include popular European artists in the existing series.

The British Council encouraged Lane's impulses by sending him on a trip, before the war had ended, to forge commercial links with South America and set up a subsidiary. After seeing to business in New York, Lane travelled down to Buenos Aires and Montevideo, meeting potential artists in countries along the way. In Mexico, he met with Señorita Ines Amor, who was to instigate a series on Mexican Modern Painters. So impressed was Lane with the flowering of art he witnessed in Mexico, that he left the country with the conviction that it was 'one of the most important art centres in the world'.

At the British Council in Montevideo, Lane was assigned a young woman by the name of Tatyana Kent, who acted as his interpreter. During a tour around the local bookshops it emerged that she had read all the first Pelicans. Impressed, Lane asked her what her ambitions were; the answer: to study at the London School of Economics. With characteristic impulsiveness, Lane offered Kent, who had never been away from the River Plate, a job at Harmondsworth. For several months after the offer nothing happened, but in September 1945 she was invited to leave Uruguay to travel to New York, stopping for a fortnight in cities along the way. The entire trip took three months, at the end of which she found herself in New York city sharing a room at the Gramercy Park Hotel with Eunice Frost. 'It was a typical Allen Lane arrangement,' she remembers. 'I had no idea what to do. I kept on writing saying please send me a list of what Penguin publishes, because I had no idea. I kept getting these letters with instructions, 'see so and so – all very important people.' Some of the people Kent met along the way were artists or critics whom Lane thought might fit into *The Penguin Modern Painters* series. In Mexico, she had to deliver a letter to the artist Siqueiros, who, unfortunately, wasn't in when she called. In Santiago she spent an hour and a half in the studio of Maria Tupper de Aguirre trying to think up appropriate comments to make while the artist showed her dozens of paintings. Kent would become Lane's secretary until her marriage to Hans Schmoller He was appointed Penguin's typographer after Jan Tschichold left the company towards the end of the 1940s – and ultimately would become a director of the company. After her wedding she became Tanya Schmoller and reduced her commitment to twelve hectic hours a week, during which she would rush about with notepad in hand, taking half-articulated instructions from Lane in taxis and lobbies or at the occasional 'weekly' meeting at Harmondsworth.

While Kent was meeting artists, Frost was in New York gathering ideas for the American, South American, Cuban and Mexican volumes. To this end she assembled an impressive cohort of American advisors: George Kubler, an expert on the history of art in the Americas; Christopher Tunnard, an architectural writer; and René d'Harancourt of the Museum of Modern Art in New York. Foremost amongst them, however, was Alfred Barr, the Director of Collections at the Museum of Modern Art. Barr was engaged as the editor for the first US monographs on Ben Shahn and Edward Hopper, and would also serve as editor for any volumes from the Americas.

The bespectacled Barr was precise, professional, and impressive; a distinguished medievalist, and a crusader in advancing the cause of artistic Modernism. As a young man he had developed America's first course in Modern Art at Harvard. Then he travelled to Asia and Europe and met the Constructivists in Russia, Mondrian's de Stijl circle in the Netherlands, and the Bauhaus in Dessau, Germany. Barr's aura of integrity was powerful enough to land him the first directorship of the Museum of Modern Art as a smooth-faced twenty-seven-year-old. It proved a wise appointment: when it came to international modern art, Barr was, arguably, better versed than Clark.

Regarding the series Barr was prolific with his opinions: 'Confining your monographs to living artists has always seemed to me rather artificial in view of the fact that a man's death is incidental to his work within his period. You deprive your readers of Sickert and publish Duncan Grant. I know Sickert is older, but he died quite recently and is three times the artist.' Among the writers Barr recommended were Gomez Sicre, Edgar Kaufmann (for a Rivera monograph) and Lincoln Kirstein (for a book on Siqueiros). He also approved Frost's suggestions for monographs on the Uruguayan artists, Figari and Torres García.

On New Year's day, 1946, Lane decided to give production a jump-start and begin the year on an expansive note. If a new series were going to be produced, the English monographs had better be taken care of, but it was also necessary to set things in motion for the international volumes. The next day he sent Clark a list of the English books then still outstanding – on Frances Hodgkins, William Nicholson, Ben Nicholson, Edward Ardizzone, and David Jones – and reviewed what stages they were at. Clark replied cheerfully, 'I was very glad to hear from you and to know that you are anxious to go ahead with *The Penguin Modern Painters*. At one time it seemed as if they were hopelessly stuck.' What Lane really intended, however, was to break to Clark his plans for a *Penguin Modern Painters* world takeover. They agreed to meet at the Travellers' Club at 4 o'clock on 22 January.

In the first stages Clark was willing to go along with the international experiment, and no doubt he could see Lane's point of view – especially when it came to European volumes. The public, 'made hungry for beauty by the necessary scarcity of war' had been fed, for practical and propagandistic reasons, almost exclusively with British art and British art books. They were now famished for international art.

Lane wasn't the only publisher to foresee the new hysteria for international culture. Other publishers, following Penguin's example, were producing slim, inexpensive volumes with attractive illustrations, only with an international angle. In 1945 Faber and Faber began The Faber Gallery series, a collection of thirty-one large paperback folios either about well-known masters, as in *Manet, Botticelli* and *Matisse*; covering artistic schools, as in *Sienese Paintings*, *Flemish Paintings*, and *Dutch Indoor Subjects*; or classified according to theme, as in *Music in Painting*, and *The Virgin and Child*. As one reviewer noted: 'Their colour plates would be hard to match even in expensive publications.'[44] The ubiquitous Kenneth Clark had his hand in the series, providing an introduction and notes for the second volume, *Florentine Paintings* (1945). Beyond a volume on Blake, 'the prophet of 'England's green and pleasant land', the series had no special emphasis on the British school.[45]

Another raft of inexpensive slim volumes, called 'Discussions on Art' was also coming onto the market. Published by Avalon, the slim monographs covered most of the European schools – with a conspicuous absence of German art – and culminated with *Byzantine Painting*. Only one book dealt with British art, and that was William Gaunt's *British Painting*, the first book in the series. Gaunt's opening volume also represented something of a closure, for although he described the 'fusion and concert among British artists' as a product of the war years and state patronage, his predictions for a new age in British art didn't translate into a new era of publishing books on the subject. This era was over.

44. A quote from *Time and Tide*, quoted from the jacket to The Faber Gallery.

45. Geoffrey Keynes, *Blake* (London: Faber and Faber, 1945), 2.

That afternoon, Clark and Lane discussed a host of possibilities. Sir Kenneth expressed some displeasure at Lane's suggestions of Portinari and Lazar Segall, for Brazil. For France, Clark agreed to consider Bonnard, but not Roualt since a book on the painter had already been published by the Museum of Modern Art. Klee would make a sensible addition, Clark believed, since plates could be photographed from the London collection. They also discussed Scandinavian artists, such as Munch, Hodin, and Sorensen from Norway, and Sandberg and Karl Hill from Sweden, and agreed that they should look into New Zealand and Cuba. Clark thought it might be worth considering Kokoschka, the German 'degenerate artist' whose art was suppressed by the Nazis; and asked to see books Lane had brought back from his travels on Figari and Argentine painters. Finally, Clark suggested that in addition to the first four US artists already scheduled for the series – namely Blume, Hopper, Davies and O'Keeffe – the artist Marin should be added. And if any English artists were to be included, Clark favoured John Tunnard, Rodrigo Moynihan, and Coldstream, although on reflection he felt there was probably not 'enough good material from Coldstream to produce the required 32 plates'.

In part, the meeting was an act of flattery on Lane's part, and a means of keeping Clark as an honorary Penguin member. Although Clark was needed to help dispense with the rest of the English monographs, with Alfred Barr and several American experts on board, it ultimately mattered little to Lane whether Clark approved of a volume on Portinari or not, and still less what his views on the US volumes were. Clark's suggestions were valuable when it came to selecting European artists and writers – but more valuable was his impressive reputation. In a sense, he had become something of a brand name, useful for the European volumes as a way of lending them authority.

Two months after his meeting with Lane, Clark had a falling-out with Peter Messer, a tall American former GI, who had taken over some of Frost's concerns during her absence in America. The details of the argument remain undisclosed, but the end result was that Clark decided to withdraw as editor of the series. No doubt the episode with Messer was merely a catalyst for feelings Clark had long been harbouring.

Frost had taken almost complete charge of editorial decisions – including choosing the artists and authors – and Clark's own input when it came to the international series carried no greater weight than that of Barr or Kubler. He was well aware he was now a backseat supporter, since it was a role he had chosen himself. But it became all too clear when the Burra and Pasmore volumes came out and no one at Penguin even thought to tell him; months later he wrote: 'I have not yet seen the published volumes on Edward Burra and Victor Pasmore but I hear them well spoken of. Perhaps you might ask a member of your staff to send me specimen copies?'

One impetus for Sir Kenneth Clark's resignation, then, was that he had certain reservations about maintaining a strictly superficial role. Furthermore, he had little time: recently he had left the National Gallery to work on writing projects of his own, including a volume for Penguin, and he was being looked at to head the Royal Fine Art Commission and the National Art Collections Fund, two duties which would use more time than he wished to think about:

I am afraid that I must give up the Editorship of *Penguin Modern Painters*. I left the Gallery in order to write books, including a very large and difficult one for you, and I am getting no writing done at all owing to numerous small commitments which pin me down at every minute of the day… it seems to me that your Modern Painters can now get on very well without me. I have given almost all the advice I am capable of giving, and the machinery can be taken on by Mr Messer or anyone else. I will do my best to push through some of the books that are outstanding, partly through my own fault, e.g. the Frances Hodgkins and the Ardizzone, and I will let you have all the material in my possession.

Clark finished on a friendly, and heartfelt note: 'I enjoyed being in at the birth of this series and I believe it has done a great service to modern painting.' Lane was not willing to let Clark slip through his fingers so easily. He wrote to Frost:

About the resignation of Kenneth Clark from the Modern Painters, I have private information (W.E.W. to wit) that he did this in a fit of pique after an interview with Messer, who I am afraid is not a born public relations man. I have deliberately done nothing in the matter as I feel sure that when you return it will be comparatively easy to talk him round. It's not the amount of work he does which is important, but as you say, it is an extremely good name to have to use as an opposite number to the Museum of Modern Art People.

Lane noted happily that, after all, it would not be long before Frost would be returning to set things aright. 'I am delighted to hear that having celebrated your first anniversary in the US, you are contemplating a visit to this country in the near future… The order for bunting has gone forth.' It is a testament to Frost's diplomatic acumen that when she returned, Clark agreed to keep his name on the monographs.

FROST'S RETURN

FROST's return heralded a new beginning in the history of *The Penguin Modern Painters*. As she had no accommodation in London, she moved into Allen Lane's house, Silverbeck, 'a solid William IV house' two miles from Harmondsworth with nine acres of garden and meadow, and half a mile of frontage on the river Colne. The floors were covered with handsome richly coloured Indian carpets brought back from a six-month foray into Asia in 1939. Morpurgo remembers Silverbeck as always being full; at the time of Frost's return, Tatyana Kent was already lodged in one of the bedrooms. After Harmondsworth had been requisitioned, Lane was obliged to treat his large home as a second office; he hired a cook and two maids to facilitate his frequent role as a host, and though it was a convivial setting for cocktail parties, dinners and receptions, all of these social gatherings were never anything but Penguin events, with printers, writers, editors and useful contacts in attendance.

One of the first things Frost may have noticed when she arrived at Silverbeck was Lane's art collection. Since the series had been initiated, Lane had made himself known at the National Gallery, Dudley Tooth's gallery and the Leicester galleries in London where the artists deposited selections of their work for him to choose from. He and his wife Lettice had also been invited to Fawley Bottom Farmhouse, John Piper's home near Henley, known as a place where guests spent idle days 'flying kites... with their doubts about themselves and their own value mysteriously stilled'.[46] There they could decide on a painting, Piper said to Lane, 'at leisure'. From the artist's point of view, Lane's most successful acquisition was a Paul Nash watercolour called, *Landscape of the Puffball*. Nash wrote to Lane expressing his delight:

> It happens to be one of my favourite drawings and while I have wondered why someone didn't perceive its quality that set it just ahead of quite a few others, I was amused to realise that there must be something – what, subversive? perhaps unwholesome about the subject. One may paint mushrooms, and I have succeeded in selling the most suspicious people pictures of palpably poisonous fungi, but puffballs, no. They seemed to be taboo. It is a great relief to me to know the spell is now broken.

Frost, though, cannot have had much time to dwell on Lane's collection at Silverbeck. She was now faced with the onerous task of sorting out the post-war mess at Harmondsworth. Expediting the English *Penguin Modern Painter* monographs that Glover and Clark had

46. Anthony West, *John Piper* (London: Secker and Warburg, 1979)

failed to get to press was only a small part of this task. She also had to push forward a new series for Australia. But drawing Frost's attention from all of these *Penguin Modern Painters* was her new passion: the addition of monographs from Latin America.

It's not surprising that Frost's attention was deflected to Latin America. Compared with the muscular group of painters she had selected after consultation with Alfred Barr and René d'Harancourt, the English Modernists looked tame. From Mexico there would be monographs on Rivera, Orozco and Siqueiros, the principal creators of the strikingly beautiful wall murals in the 1920s that had sparked off the formidable renaissance of art in Mexico which had so impressed Lane. Diego Rivera's reputation has since been overshadowed by that of his wife, Frida Kahlo, but at the time the sixty-year-old was an artistic giant, known for splendid panoramas that were rich with human and archaeological detail, rife with political zeal, and unabashedly realistic. An avowed communist, Rivera had housed Trotsky in his low blue house in Mexico until the exiled communist's affair with his wife Frida was discovered.

Orozco was famous for his violent statements in fresco: such as Christ as a militant revolutionary butchering his cross with an axe. By some he was considered to be the 'El Greco of Mexico'. The youngest of the triumvirate was David Alfaro Siqueiros who created monumental baroque compositions, full of heroes, demons, and centaurs of the Conquest. It was a formidable line-up. At a time when *pistoleros* were assassinating politically inclined writers and artists in broad daylight, Barr and Frost decided against using Mexican authors for political reasons: 'It could simplify what might otherwise be a particularly complicated local situation [to]... find writers for the Orozco, Rivera and Siqueiros volumes with international understanding of art.'

Barr had also agreed to George Kubler's suggestion for a volume on the Brazilian master, Portinari, the author of earthy coffee-coloured scenes of his native São Paulo, and portraits so telling of the subjects' characters that you could almost see them gesture and speak. In 1933, as a poor unknown artist, Portinari had torn strips from the hand-woven linen sheets of his new wife's heirloom, and destroyed the upholstery on his family's coveted colonial furniture as a substitute for the canvas he could not afford. His perseverance paid off: by 1939, he had staged a one-man exhibition at the National Museum of Fine Arts in Rio de Janeiro, and had been a representative at the Brazilian Pavilion at the New York World Fair. He was considered a great master for his Modernist murals – dealing with Brazilian social themes – and his Expressionist paintings which drew attention to poverty and injustice in northeast Brazil.

From Uruguay, Barr and Frost planned a volume on Figari. Finally, there was to be a departure from the monograph formula with a composite volume on Cuban artists: Wilfredo Lam, Amelia Pelaez, Ponce de Leon, Victor Manuel, Ravenet, Carlos Enriques, Mariano, Portocarrero, Carreno, Cundo, and Moreno. Alfred Barr supported the Cuban proposal – 'We have I think much the best collection of Cuban painting anywhere' – but he was displeased with Frost's choice of author, Guy Pérez Cisneros, a member of the Cuban delegation to the United Nations: 'Cisneros is a rather pedantic, scholarly critic with no great taste and unfortunately with some political connections.' Each Cuban was allocated two or three colour and black-and-white reproductions, but the format was to follow the usual for the series, with a single introductory essay and a total of sixteen colour and sixteen black and white plates.

Amazingly, only one of these volumes came to fruition: the one on Portinari. Mexico posed difficulties because most of the paintings were murals: difficult to photograph, and more difficult to reproduce. 'As in a number of cases the subject consists of a mural painting,' Lane wrote to their Mexican contact, Ines Amor, 'it is desirable that one should work as close to the subject as possible, but are there any four-colour process engravers of the quality we want in Mexico?' Indeed, there were not, and with a bottleneck in engraving in New York, there was no chance of producing the monographs in America. Back in England the situation was worse; with war-weariness, and continuing labour and material shortages, the handicaps imposed by the Blitz and war-time conditions had not lifted, but printers were expected to cope with the surge of trade which accompanied the end of wartime hostilities. Frost wrote to Amor: 'The unfortunate thing is that printing conditions over here have become increasingly worse, and are now even more complicated by the fuel and power shortages so that many things have had to mark time.' For the non-appearance of the Cuban volume, Frost would attribute some of the blame to Cisneros: 'Between you and me,' she complained to Penguin's New York representative, '[Cisneros] has the trait of all Latin Americans of remoteness from reality.'

Figari came much closer to press, and a shipment of paintings was even dispatched to England for plate-making. In October Frost wrote to Barr about her thoughts on the collection:

> I find most of the Figaris that have been sent here very disappointing examples, and I would not be happy to have him represented inadequately, which I think would be the case if we used the material which came from Giselda Zani, but which is by no means his best. I have planned though to make the best selection I can for colour and reselect the black and white entirely. I had hoped to get the Arts Council to do a Figari exhibition, but I am afraid their committee rejected it after seeing our collection of paintings.

She was also disappointed with the text, which had been written by Giselda Zani, the author of a monograph on Figari published in Buenos Aires in 1944: 'Apart from matters of fact, I did find [Zani's text] over lyrical, but this requires a pruning and a restraint with which she may find it difficult to agree.' Still, two years later, Frost had a dummy of the Figari volume in hand, and Tanya Schmoller remembers seeing proofs. Whatever happened to this monograph remains a mystery.

Far from being a case of the 'remoteness from reality' of Latin Americans, the Portinari volume owes its existence to the fact that when it came to plates, the Brazilians were largely impervious to Frost's meddling. The monograph was brought out in conjunction with Penguin's associated firm in Rio de Janeiro, Editora y Distribuidora Penguin Ltda: 'They are undertaking, out there, the production of sixteen colour plates and sixteen black and white plates, and will ship the plates to us here so that we can print the book in England to form one in our series of contemporary artists both British, Australian, New Zealand, American and Latin America.' The Rio firm intended the monograph as the first in a series called Arte no Brasil, edited by Lelio Landucci.

In September, Frost went to Paris to meet Portinari who had an exhibition: 'I must tell you how very much I enjoyed meeting you, your wife and small boy. It was certainly one of the most pleasant evenings I had while in Paris, and I was particularly glad to have the chance of seeing so much of your work.' Soon after, she could report that 'the Portinari volume is at present printing'. More information however, she could not provide, since the Rio firm, despite insistent cabling from England, neglected to send proofs of the black and white and colour plates, or a copy of the text itself. The original text was written by Anibal Machado, who was, in the words of the Rio office: 'one of our best art critics'. The firm reported: 'The technique of galvanoplastics has been employed in order to provide perfect rendition of the pictures, even after the printing of 25,000 copies of the book.' As for the proofs: 'We regret not to let you have now the proofs for all colour plates. They are needed by the printers.'

The next year, Eunice Frost got a copy of the text – in French – and sent it off to a recent acquaintance, the notoriously difficult art impresario, Douglas Cooper. He replied:

> I have read it: the pleasure was not great. The French used is 'colonial' in quality. As a text it says nothing of interest. It does not deal with Portinari's work, except in terms of such jungle magic as would seem appropriate to a Brazilian setting. He becomes willy-nilly a figure of fun, for no one could live up to the majority of statements made. I don't know him, so I can't tell how he is – but priggishness is not a pleasing quality. I wouldn't recommend this text in English.

Like the Figari text, it was a conflict between English understatement and Latin style. In the end, English understatement won out. The Machado text was replaced with an introduction by Lelio Landucci, the book's editor. Visually, the Portinari volume had a distinctly different flavour from the English, American and French monographs, and it was never sold in the UK. The book is slightly larger (23.5 x 20cms), with a plain grey-blue front, and white rear cover. A rather muscular penguin stands menacingly on a stylised iceberg between the words EDIÇÕES and PINGUIM on the front, and centred on the rear. The title is in a heavy Bodoni face, coloured brown. Inside, the book follows the usual format, but the colour plates are of varying quality, with some muted and slightly indistinct.

WORKING WITH AMERICA

THE history of the two American *Penguin Modern Painters* – Ben Shahn and Edward Hopper – is interesting insofar as it throws light on the relations between Allen Lane and the New York branch of Penguin Books, which progressed rapidly from tenuous to inoperable. When Allen Lane chose Kurt Enoch and, later, Victor Weybright, to head Penguin Books International (PBI), he chose two people in his own image – headstrong, ambitious and possessing a flair for publishing. Neither was likely to submit to the authoritarian rule with which Lane was apt to run his business, and Weybright in particular didn't appreciate his plans for adapting Penguin Books to the US market hampered by what he viewed as Lane's middle-class English conservatism. Weybright regarded Lane as an 'exceptional country boy in the big city', endowed with energy, charm and brains, but with too much 'vicarage garden prudery' to figure out what might go down well in the new world. Lane, for his part, viewed some of Weybright's proposals as racy, and held fears, perhaps exaggerated ones, that the Penguin operation in America might 'waft bad odours' back to England. He continuously enlisted Weybright to act as an informer on Enoch, but this strategy backfired and only impelled the American collaborators (who were initially mutually suspicious) to work in closer accord.

After editorial content, the major bone of contention between the US collaborators and Lane was over presentation. Paperbacks in America were sold not only in traditional bookshops, but through magazine outlets, where they could command enormous sales. To attract interest, many had pictorial covers, some with loosely clad women and intonations of sexual desire. These incurred the wrath of Allen Lane and his brother Richard, and in *The Penguin Story*, W.E. Williams would write that American publishers reached sales on a massive scale, because they treated books as 'a commodity with garish and sensational eye appeal'. Lane held tightly to the idea that typographical book covers reinforced Penguin's identity, and that people would buy books for the imprint, not for the picture on the cover. However, this was far truer in Britain than in the US market.

The design dispute came to a head over the *Modern Painters*, not primarily because Weybright and others advocated picture covers, but because they saw the typographical layout as 'more Edwardian than modern'. Modern and attractive art monographs from the continent were flooding the New York market, and the novel appeal of *The Penguin Modern Painters* was beginning to fade. Weybright wrote to Lane expressing his hope that their first joint art project, American Modern Painters, would 'excel in distinction and consistency over everything in the field at any given price'.

Weybright was strongly supported by Alfred Barr. In July 1945, the Director of the Museum of Modern Art wrote a very polite memorandum to Penguin urging them to update their typography, but much later, he regarded the changes they had made as entirely superficial. His suggestions were not unreasonable, but Harmondsworth found them unacceptable. There was, of course, an element of British pride and prejudice against US standards in their resistance. Barr, who had knowledge of current trends in art-book publishing wrote lengthy, pleading letters, but with little effect:

> I can do little but remind you of my memorandum of July 24, 1945, now over a year and a half old, and urge you again to revise your typography and layout radically. I can't tell you exactly what to do because I am not a typographer, but I would be inclined to abandon the strict symmetry with its resultant inorganic 'hour-glass', and change the colour of the jacket from the cream and ochre combination to something handsomer and less soilable… Let me urge you strongly once more to save two valuable pages by omitting the list of plates, using instead somewhat longer captions which should be carefully laid out in relation to the cuts. If… you feel you absolutely have to have the list of plates, may I urge you to number them in sequence rather than establishing a separate table of contents for color and then for the black and white.

He concluded, 'so far as the American market is concerned, a modernized typography and layout would be a real help both esthetically and commercially'.

Barr's suggestions met with continued antipathy from the UK. Since the books were being produced and printed in England, ultimately, Harmondsworth held the reins of control. Eventually, Eunice Frost agreed to make two editions – one for the US and one for England with differing typographical layouts. She also agreed to redesign the cover to something less 'soilable' and put before Clark the idea of having separate colours to distinguish American, Australian and Latin American editions. But the war over typography continued apace.

Over the next two years, except for the change of cover design – which was extended to the other volumes in the series – every one of Barr and Victor Weybright's recommendations for typographical change were greeted dilatorily. For the Shahn volume, Harmondsworth can perhaps be excused: a major exhibition at the New York MoMA was scheduled for May 1947, and the book had to be issued in time for the opening. The huge backlog amongst New York engravers meant that all of the plates had to be made in England in the course of a few months – a monumental task which took time and resources away from the British monographs. Early in 1947, Frost agreed to consider the use of American designers for the US edition, but when Weybright and Barr sent Frost a new sleek typographical layout by the designer Robert Josephy, she sent the first volume on Ben Shahn to press with the old layout. 'I must warn you,' she wrote to Barr after the printing, 'it was impossible to wait longer to receive the

Josephy typographical layout so we had to go ahead with a revised version of the text and prelims.' Barr's frustration, and Weybright's feeling of powerlessness were palpable. 'I must say I was shocked to see what a highly impractical and awkward typographical layout had been used,' wrote Barr:

> You know that for three years now I have been urging a type reform in the Penguin art series books but the sight of these makes me throw up my hands. At least you must align the captions to the left as you have already done in some of the previous books so that the numbers will come one above the other.
>
> I suppose I am wasting time repeating that I think these two pages given over to the listing of plates is an extravagant error, considering the paper shortage and space shortage. The inclusion of this two-page list forces us to omit the really useful lists which we had prepared to follow the text, namely, the reading list, the list of murals in public buildings, of one-man shows and of paintings in museums. You have the final word in this but I shall never stop protesting.

To Weybright, Barr sent a letter that revealed his feelings about the Shahn monograph:

> I suppose that you have now seen a copy of the Ben Shahn. The color plates were quite good, the typography what we expected from the proofs, except for the fact that there is a bastard title, Page 17, with a single magic word 'Plates' in 16-point, followed by a verso absolutely blank. This is the last straw, even worse than the perfectly stupid typography of pages 19 and 20... I don't know what to do about this. It seems to me that Eunice Frost was more helpless than careless, and Lane too busy.

The choice of colour, he said, was 'rather grim'. 'I believe Arthur Symons would have called it a "sad French green".' Barr concluded angrily: 'I am afraid I am cynical enough to believe that what seems impossible to [Frost] is the result more of unwillingness to do something new than the cost or a sense of fair play.'

Weybright was equally aggrieved: 'I realize PBL is the publisher with primary responsibility, but PBI has assumed that we were not entirely silent partners in this venture... The acceptability of the book by American readers does not, as Frostie sometimes imagines, mean its complete Americanization. The modern touch is a universal one, and that is what Barr has been striving for.'

In fairness to Frost, the Shahn volume had been a tremendous effort to produce at all, a point hardly understood by PBI. In order to entice American collectors to loan their Shahn paintings to Penguin, Frost had gone to great lengths to arrange an exhibition of Shahn's work at the Mayor Gallery in Brook Street, after which the paintings travelled to Brighton Art Gallery, and subsequently to Bristol. Supplies of art paper were still severely depleted, and, as Richard Lane wrote to Weybright in his defence, post-war economy meant that Harmondsworth was 'having to work with a typographer not only unsympathetic towards being accommodating towards the American point of view, but even towards our own'. Indeed, the struggle to meet the deadline for the Shahn exhibition in New York imperilled Frost's programme for the English Modern

Painters. A final cloud over the Shahn book occurred when Enoch tried to unload costs onto the UK headquarters and disputed the published price of 3/6d, an increase over the 2/6d cost of earlier volumes. For the first time ever, Frost's letters took on a personal tone and she admitted to feeling 'rather hurt'. 'I cannot imagine that the Museum could have produced and published it themselves with such speed, or at such a price,' she concluded, 'it must relieve their programme quite a considerable amount to know that their members' book, to co-incide with the Shahn exhibition, is being supplied by us.'

The Ben Shahn volume brought the hitherto unheard of American artist to the galleries of Britain and future volumes contained new, more modern typography. Some British book-buyers regarded the new volume with suspicion and unease, but Frost sent these individuals letters to pique their interest in the new series: 'It may be that you do not care particularly for the sociological implications in Ben Shahn's work. Perhaps, though, you will like better the Edward Hopper, the next artist we have selected, or Georgia O'Keefe, Peter Blume and John Marin (only the Hopper was produced). At least one important figure in the British art world, however, was genuinely impressed with the Shahn book: 'A r. good choice to introduce American art,' wrote Clark to Frost encouragingly. 'It makes Spencer look strangely insular.'

By January 1948, relations between the American and British Penguins were in shambles, and a breach was imminent. The negotiations between Lane and Weybright took nearly a week, with Frost and Williams watching miserably from the sidelines. It would not bode well for the new series in hand. 'We are still enormously anxious to go on with the American Modern Painters, as well as the Mexicans,' Frost rushed off in a note to Alfred Barr: 'This separation is all very sad, especially at a time when one wants all the understanding in the world that one can achieve, but can it be that the type of standards that we are constantly striving for here in our editorial and production work are not really right for America?' As seen, the difficulties were indeed insurmountable, and only Hopper, already far advanced in production would grace the bookshop displays of the Museum of Modern Art. Weybright, in the meantime, founded Signet, an imprint with no interest in producing art monographs.

THE NEW PENGUIN TYPOGRAPHY

IT would be entirely fallacious to believe that Allen Lane wasn't concerned with the presentation of his books. He was spontaneous, given to bold and rash ideas. But he was also territorial, and fiercely self-protective. This peculiar combination of personality traits prevented him from opening Penguin to the typographical suggestions of the American branch, even if these suggestions had made good commercial sense. But it is some indication of his profound interest in the design of his books that he invited Europe's most famous typographer to join Penguin.

There are several variants of the story of how the German typographer Jan Tschichold came to work at Penguin. The best one is related by Morpurgo in his biography of Lane:

> One day in 1947 – so runs the story – Allen was lunching with Oliver Simon, one of the greatest English book designers. In a way that was undoubtedly typical, he asked a number of direct questions, among them: 'Who do you think is the best typographer in the world?' Answer: Jan Tschichold, a German living and working in Switzerland. 'Can we get him?' Almost before his friend had completed an expressive shrug Allen was at the telephone calling, first, Tschichold in Switzerland and then an air-taxi service. Within twenty-four hours he had contracted Tschichold to come to England.

The story is certainly exaggerated, since in response to a query to Barr in March 1947, Frost wrote: 'While it is true that Jan Tschichold is coming to us, this will not be for a little time to come and it was not really practicable to ask him to restyle the Modern Painters, we felt, before he officially joined us.' According to Ruari McLean, author of *Jan Tschichold, Typographer* (1990), 'Allen Lane and Oliver Simon flew to Basle in September 1946 and invited Tschichold to come to England and become the Penguin typographer. He accepted but was not able to give up his Swiss commitments and come to London until March 1947.'

Photographs of Tschichold show a man whose elegance betrays his flair for spacing and typefaces. He looks meticulous even in monochrome. Tschichold was the son of a sign painter and studied at the Academy of Book Design, Leipzig. In the 1920s he wrote an article 'Elementare Typographie' (*Typographische Mitteilungen,* Oct. 1925) and a book *Die neue Typographie* (Berlin, 1928) in which he advocated sans serif typefaces and asymmetrical layouts. Before the Second World War, he fled Germany to work in Switzerland. To his astonishment and horror, he realised that there existed the most shocking parallels between his earlier teachings and the totalitarian regimes of National Socialism and Fascism.

His consequent *volte-face* alienated many of his former acolytes, but boded well for Penguin, where he fashioned symmetrical designs and promoted the use of serif typefaces for their legibility.

Before arriving in England Tschichold requested a sample of every book cover produced by Penguin. These he annotated in pencil and sent back to the firm. The designers and typesetters were astonished by his skill. So highly regarded was his work that Allen Lane paid him a salary higher than his and Dick's combined. By Tschichold's own account, in the twenty-nine months he was at Penguin he 'designed or prepared for press more than 500 books, mostly page by page, which must be nearly a world record'.[47]

Tschichold's magical touch was first applied to *The Penguin Modern Painters* in the volumes *William Nicholson, Ben Nicholson, Frances Hodgkins* and *David Jones,* upon whose covers the dancing penguin device was now set against a white circle, and a finer lettering was used for both the series' title and the name of the artist. These alterations were probably not made directly by Tschichold, but made following his annotations to earlier volumes sent from Switzerland, and indeed, major inconsistencies in formatting between the volumes abound. The first edition of *Paul Klee* published in 1949, however, is unmistakably Tschichold; on this cover the series' title appears in an attractive and more cursive font, and Tschichold's redrawn upright Penguin encircled by two white lines, has replaced the device Williams once described as 'a Penguin in the throes of appendicitis'.[48] The colour of the cover is a sophisticated grey-blue, instead of the chocolate-brown that Frost had selected in 1947. *Paul Klee* was selected by the National Book League as one of the best designed books of the year. The new standard was applied to subsequent numbers including the 1951 reprint of *Henry Moore, Edward Hopper* (1949), and *Ivon Hitchens* (1955). *Edward Hopper,* of course, differed because, at the behest of the American collaborators, it included a reading list, and listed the plates in the order in which they appeared rather than in separate lists according to whether they were colour or black-and-white. (*William Nicholson,* likewise bears the effects of the efforts of the Americans since his plates are also listed in the order in which they appear.) Ivon Hitchens wished for what he called a 'dingy blue' blue to be replaced with a bright blue cover, since 'public taste has become keyed up to a very bright range of colours'. However, in this instance, Penguin held its course.

Despite Tschichold's efforts to standardise, even after the design was formalised in 1949, there were differences in the presentation of the captions. Tschichold aimed at uniformity, but with up to three companies involved in the production of any given book, and the

47. Quoted in Ruari McLean, *Jan Tshichold, Typographer* (London: Lund Humphries, 1990), 144.

48. Sir William Emrys Williams, *The Penguin Story*, (Harmondsworth: Penguin,1956), 25.

impossibility of making personal calls to these companies, such variations were inevitable. In an essay entitled 'My Reform of Penguin Books' (*Schweizer Graphische Mitteilungen*, No. 6, 1950), reproduced in McLean's book, Tschichold recalled what it was like to work for England's largest publisher:

> Penguin Books use a large number of printing and binding firms all over the British Isles. Distances are so great that visits even to a firm in London are only occasionally possible: any visit takes nearly a whole day, most of which is spent in travelling. Corrections can hardly be made quickly. In exceptional circumstances, they may be made within a week, but more often it takes weeks or even months before one can see a revise. These delays do not make a typographer's life any easier.

This partly explains why there were so many delays in producing *The Penguin Modern Painters* series, which involved not only straightforward text, but lists of plates, colour reproductions, monochromes, and captions too. It also may explain, for example, why *Ben Nicholson* stands out, with a different title-page verso from that of *Frances Hodgkins* and the reprint of *Paul Nash*. (*Ben Nicholson* is also the only volume with an italic lower-case sans-serif font for the captions.)

Aside from their gentle differences, the *Penguin Modern Painters* that appeared after Tschichold's arrival were a great improvement over both *Ben Shahn* and *Stanley Spencer*, and the first eight numbers with their 'soilable' golden-cream and white covers. The series was now truly modern.

THE AUSTRALIANS

IT is perhaps strange to write a history of something that doesn't exist. We may well imagine the Australian *Penguin Modern Painters*, their reproductions expressing the forlorn emptiness of incandescent Australian skies, heat scorched soil, broken-down townships, and the lean bodies of men leaning against the ragged posts of old hotels. We may envision these books with their covers in card of a certain periwinkle blue and printed with typography by Jan Tschichold. But these lovely volumes were prevented from entering the world through the pride and stubbornness of those very individuals supposedly responsible for their creation.

The history of these non-existent volumes had its inauspicious start at the meeting between Clark and Lane at the Travellers' Club, when, try as he might, Clark was unable to remember the names of two good Australian painters he had heard of from the Melbourne media-magnate Sir Keith Murdoch. He promised to send the names to Lane by post.

The two artists were William Dobell and Russell Drysdale, painters who could not have been better suited for the series. Dobell had mixed in the Slade circles in London as a young man, and had studied, like Paul Nash, Ben Nicholson and Stanley Spencer, under the supervision of Henry Tonks. The two Australians had also served as official Australian War Artists, and Drysdale's sketches of soldiers resting and men asleep on the platforms of train stations, recall Moore's Underground sketches. It is not surprising that Kenneth Clark would later advise that monographs on these artists be pursued on purely 'artistic grounds' regardless of their commercial value.

Again, like the other *Penguin Modern Painters*, Dobell and Drysdale were heavily influenced by European Modernists but, arguably, they were up against even greater obstacles when it came to establishing their reputations. Galleries in Australia were 'Augean stables', full of pictures of fleece and gum-trees and overrun by prudish trustees. The Director of the National Gallery of Victoria once pronounced: 'I don't think we should have modern art in the Gallery at all. It is not liked by the Art Galleries of Australia.' The supreme attraction of the Melbourne Gallery was a stuffed horse named Phar Lap, believed locally to be the best race-horse of all time.

Artists wanting to experiment in the modernist tradition suffered in this hostile climate. The prestigious Archibald Prize for 1943 (awarded in January 1944) was won by Dobell's painting *Joshua Smith*, a portrait of his artist friend. The painting showed Smith almost as if viewed in a hall of mirrors: his neck was elongated, his hands were strangely oversized, and one eye had an unsettling droop. To anyone even vaguely familiar with German New Realism of the 1920s, the portrait would have seemed entirely within the limits of convention. But to two disgruntled contestants, it was outrageous enough to take Dobell and the Archibald Trustees to court. The charge was that the painting was a caricature and not a portrait at all: the court sensibly judged in Dobell's favour.

Early in 1946, while Frost was away in America, Peter Messer put plans for the Australian series in motion. One of his associates had just returned from Sydney, bringing word of a gentleman by the name of Sydney Ure Smith, an English-born publisher who had developed a good reputation for his 'missionary' work on behalf of the generation of young Australian artists coming of age under the influence of Picasso and Braque. A photo-portrait of Ure Smith in the catalogue to 'The Sydney Ure Smith Memorial Exhibition' shows him in a dark three-piece suit, glowering at the camera, his fingers curled around an unlit pipe; in the backwoods climate of Australia, he must have cut an imposing, if incongruous figure. In any event, he seemed the perfect partner for Penguin: his company, Ure Smith Pty Limited produced attractive slim volumes on the work of young Australians – counterparts to *The Penguin Modern Painters* – which were said to have had a good educational effect and set a new standard in Australian book production. And in 1917, he began publishing the magazine *Art in Australia*.

Correspondence between Peter Messer and the august publisher quickly led to an informal agreement in which Sidney Ure Smith was commissioned to oversee the production of the Australian volumes. Both sides were ecstatic: 'So glad to have such quick replies to my letters to you – also it makes me "step on it",' Ure Smith wrote. For his part, Messer regarded Ure Smith with optimism and admiration. 'From his letters he seems a very sincere person,' Messer informed Penguin's Melbourne representative, Bob Maynard. 'He has been most enthusiastic about the whole scheme and most helpful.'

The rapport strengthened until Frost returned to England and Messer left Penguin Books to join Weybright in his native America. With the admiring Messer gone, and Frost overworked and harassed and carrying far too much on her delicate shoulders, relations between Penguin and the Australian publisher began to go awry.

Ostensibly, the dispute between Frost and Ure Smith revolved around the provision of colour plates for the books, though there was also some turmoil over the choice of authors. As for the plates, Ure Smith offered to have them engraved in Australia, so that he could use them for his own publications; he was just then preparing a comprehensive pictorial record of Dobell's career including 102 reproductions. Frost, on the other hand, insisted that his plates were either inadequate or too large for the Penguin books, and requested that Ure Smith ship the paintings to England so that they could be made there and the proofs checked against the originals. In Frost's favour, it could be argued that the Ure Smith plates did not conform exactly to the measurements she had provided. Conversely, it should be noted that his reproductions were not sub-standard at all. Very quickly the dispute escalated into a power struggle over who had ultimate control over the production of the books, with Ure Smith resorting to subterfuge, and Frost responding with an infuriating silence.

Ure Smith's main strategy was endlessly to put off shipping the paintings. 'I have been such a mass of indecision over the sending of the paintings,' he wrote to Frost in February 1947, 'and Dobell was away and I wished to consult him over the matter.' The problem, claimed Ure Smith, was the interminable shipping and waterfront strikes. 'The prospect of the Dobell pictures… sitting on a wharf for some time awaiting shipment in Sydney dismays one,' he complained. 'I am wondering if, after all, it would be possible to use the originals of my colour blocks, and if necessary get some new ones engraved here. It would save endless trouble and expense and I think the actual blocks are very good…' Frost, who had made gestures towards getting an import licence, was furious, dismissed Ure Smith as inept, and decided that his age and ill-health precluded the need to correspond with him further.

For the next few months Ure Smith wrote to Frost regularly and desperately. Not receiving any answer, he forged ahead with his plans for the Penguins, had blocks engraved, sent invoices to Penguin and discussed the choice of paintings with the artists. He also made overtures to the writers Bryan Penton and Bernard Smith for the Drysdale book and Professor Joseph Burke for Dobell. In his agitated correspondence to Frost, his version of events changed with each letter. First he said that Messer had authorised him to make all the colour blocks himself. Then he admitted the plan to send paintings had been scrapped (by himself, of course) owing to strikes and delays in shipping. In all the letters he admonished Frost; he compared her conduct unfavourably with that of Messer; he insistently reminded her that although he had sent her letters by *air mail* she had not bothered to reply.

By any yardstick, Frost's unannounced dismissal of Ure Smith was discourteous. In Frost's defence, it should be pointed out that she was also struggling with volumes on five American, three Mexican, one Brazilian, one goup of Cubans and one French artist, as well as looking after the entire Penguin fiction list, and attending to *Science News* and *Penguin's Progress*. She had found Harmondsworth in a state of complete disarray after returning from America, especially with all the disorientating staff changes. Not only that, she was living at Silverbeck, so Penguin was a continual preoccupation. Meanwhile, England had not yet recovered from the war, and the populace had to rely on food parcels from abroad to supplement meagre rations.

In the autumn Bob Maynard took a trip to Sydney and discovered Ure Smith 'frightfully narked' and next to distraught over the Penguins. Ure Smith's own health was precarious, but he nonetheless felt compelled to honour his commitment to Penguin. He had come to regard himself as the managing editor of the Australian series, and felt disempowered by the lack of signals arriving from Harmondsworth. In a desperate attempt to agree the authors and have the plates made, he appealed to Maynard to intercede. Frost's response to Maynard's report was terse: 'If you should be seeing Ure Smith again, you might calm him down, if he really needs it, by pointing out that at our present rate of production it is taking anything up to two years to get a *Modern Painter* through.' Despite such hints, Ure Smith's frantic letters continued, as did Frost's feigned ignorance of them.

Early in 1948 Frost considered abandoning the Australian series. The burden of work was greater than she could manage, her health was fragile, and every fresh letter from Ure Smith jangled her nerves. Furthermore, sales of British *Penguin Modern Painters* were waning, so print runs were diminishing and the price of each issue would have to be raised. Frost was growing sceptical of the sort of reception the books might receive in Australia, and besides, Glover, Williams and Lane had apparently lost all interest. The final straw occurred when Ure Smith delivered a well-aimed jab in a letter to Harmondsworth, which cast her in a none too favourable light. Frost wrote to Clark suggesting that perhaps the Australian series wasn't such a good idea after all.

Clark was horrified and immediately took the side of the Australian publisher: 'Your letter is rather disturbing, because people in Australia are perfectly confident that you are going to do Penguin Books on Drysdale and Dobell, and have prepared all the material.' Sensibly, he advised Frost to use the Australian plates and be done with it: 'From the point of view of quality it appeared that the plates in the latest Ure Smith publications... were just about as good as those which we produced.'

That summer, Frost's interest in the series were rekindled. A young woman called Lucy Swanton, who ran the Macquarie Galleries in Sydney, arrived in London with two Drysdale paintings. Frost was charmed by her; they had friends in common in London, and Swanton said she utterly agreed with Frost about the quality of the Ure Smith blocks. In order to excite Drysdale's personal enthusiasm for bringing his work to England, the two worked up a scheme to get the work of both artists exhibited at the Tate. If the plan worked, Frost believed, it would also drum up enough of an audience to justify publishing the books, the majority of which were to be sold in England. By the time Swanton left England, she and Frost were fast friends, with Swanton writing Frost warm letters from her tour of Europe: 'Paris has kept me in an almost constant simmer of excitement so perhaps it is as well I am going to have a few weeks rusticating in the south before being faced with the glories of Italy.'

Back in Australia, Swanton started assembling paintings for shipment in the back room of the Macquarie Galleries. Drysdale was excited at the prospect of his work going to London, and Swanton was equally pleased at the effect of this new-found optimism on his work. 'Now, this couldn't be better because it means also that he will swing straight into a painting mood and may easily surpass anything he has previously done,' she wrote to Frost. Dobell was another matter, and would be more difficult to curry favour with. Maynard reported that Dobell had shut himself away up the New South Wales coast, and 'refuses to see anybody, and has apparently given up painting completely. Could one call it tempera-mental?' he suggested.

Richard Lane, now also in Australia, proved ineffectual in resolving the business, and Ure Smith grew too ill to discuss the Australian editions. Maynard and Frost conspired to cut Ure Smith out of the picture. Maynard wrote: 'The last time I saw Gwen Spencer – Ure Smith's winger – she was bemoaning the fact that we were doing all the dallying on these two books. I do not know to what extent you are committed to Smith, but I would like to see them taken completely away.' One problem remained, and that was Ure Smith's close friendship with the artists. To drop him entirely might antagonise Drysdale, and the publisher's reaction was certain to upset the temperamental Dobell. Frost settled on a compromise: to use three of Ure Smith's blocks and tactfully suggest that it might ease matters from his point of view if they were to enrol the personal help of Miss Swanton for the shipment and selection of paintings. In the meantime, Maynard and Frost set up correspondence about possible authors for the volumes without consulting Ure Smith: 'Turnbull would be quite good for Drysdale,' wrote Maynard, 'I do not know about Haefliger, but will find what I can. Crawford should be quite good for Dobell.'

In 1947 Sir Kenneth Clark arrived in Australia. If anyone were to doubt the humour and strength of personality of the man, they would do well to read his account of the trip in his autobiography, *The Other Half*. Clark was invited to Australia by the Melbourne Gallery, for which he acted as a purchase advisor. The purpose of the trip was to assess their needs, which, as Clark writes, 'were in fact what they saw reproduced in the fashionable art magazines'. On the passage over, Sir Kenneth was besieged by women of questionable motives, and developed a bad reputation for having stumped the ship's medium. When he arrived in Australia, he discovered 'a race of gods', a non-hypocritical people with 'magnificent physiques'. He also discovered a breed of talented young artists, some of whom inspired his patronage and support.

Being disinclined to drag Clark into one of Penguin's 'little brawls', Maynard neglected to set up a meeting with Ure Smith. Plans had been made, however, for Clark to meet the artists and to see their work at the Macquarie Galleries. At that point Clark was to assess the list of pictures for the books and add his own favourites to the selection. The meeting proved especially fortuitous for Drysdale. As Swanton wrote to Frost: 'I expect Sir Kenneth Clark will have arrived by this time and told you that he met Drysdale, saw his things and also bought an important painting which was all very exciting and stimulating for the artist.' He also suggested an exhibition of paintings at the Leicester Galleries in London, which was perhaps a more realistic option than showing them at the Tate. Miss Swanton was delighted.

Despite Maynard's wishes, Clark got entangled in the publishing drama. In January, he travelled to Sydney with Professor Joseph Burke, Ure Smith's chosen author for the Drysdale book, and the two of them dropped in on the publisher. They discovered Ure Smith full of impatience and ire. As he thundered in an antagonistic four-page letter to Frost: 'I saw Sir Kenneth about all the difficulties regarding these two books and he promised to take the matter up with you when he went back.' Clark indeed took Ure Smith's side, but not because he necessarily believed him. He had visited Australia as an ambassador, and as editor of the series; he feared losing face if the monographs weren't produced. When he arrived in London he beseeched Frost to co-operate and talked of the 'bewilderment and disappointment' there would be if Penguin didn't continue with them after all the plans that had been made. Frost held her ground: 'I am inclined to suggest that we compromise by collaborating with Miss Swanton for Drysdale and Ure Smith about Dobell. Even though the latter will be intolerable, I am sure.' To Swanton she wrote: '[Ure Smith] seems to be under the impression that he is to handle the matter [of the Australian series]'.

As the monographs continued to stagnate, both Frost's and Ure Smith's health deteriorated. Frost spent most of early 1949 in bed, ignoring correspondence, prompting Alfred Barr to write to Allen Lane: 'I am under increasing embarrassment here because of the extraordinary delay I have to suffer from Eunice's failure to answer letters.' In March her doctor ordered her to take a minimum leave of one month in Switzerland. 'I am pretty confident that after all, we shall not have to abandon the Drysdale-Dobell project, but only have it postponed until I am fully fit enough to deal with the whole thing,' she wrote to Swanton optimistically. 'The whole thing will just have to be held up until I am well again.' To Ure Smith, she wrote a letter ascribing the delays to his own illness, 'the standard of some of the blocks', and his inability to collect the material for shipping. 'And now, as you will have heard, it is my turn to plead sickness.' Frost never bothered writing to Ure Smith again, and it was Christmas before even Swanton would hear from her.

Late in 1949 Ure Smith died suddenly: according to a letter from his assistant, Miss Spencer, he had been in the midst of drafting a letter to Allen Lane about the difficulties of working with Penguin. Lane replied: 'I think the least we can do is to give you the permission for which you now ask, and you can take this letter as being our authorisation on this point.' He also thanked her for sending him a copy of the catalogue, produced by the Australian publishers, to a memorial exhibition celebrating the outstanding work of Sydney Ure Smith: '[It] seems to me to be very well produced.'

The Australian books were never published. The Drysdale plates made their way into a 1950 Ure Smith volume on the artist with an essay by Joseph Burke. Ure

Smith's 1946 volume *William Dobell*, by Brian Penton, seems to have been mooted for inclusion in the Ure Smith miniature series, but it never appeared. In December 1950, Sir Kenneth Clark orchestrated a large exhibition of work by Russell Drysdale at the Leicester Galleries which helped re-establish Australian art's beleaguered reputation and revealed a new landscape fantastic to the British eye. The show, which Drysdale attended with his wife and children, was a success both financially and critically. As a consequence of the exhibition his painting, 'War Memorial' – depicting a cheap cast statue looking 'unreal and out of key' in a small bush community – was purchased out of the Knapping Fund for the collection of the Tate Gallery.[49]

49. Ronald Alley, *Catalogue of The Tate Gallery's Collection of Modern Art Other than Works by British Artists*, (London: Tate Gallery, 1981), 179.

KLEE

WHEN Kenneth Clark advocated a volume on Klee for *The Penguin Modern Painters*, he was proving his mastery of the formulae for a successful art monograph: precede publication with a popular exhibition of the artist's work, and take advantage of having the paintings in one place to make plates. In 1945, the Tate Gallery had held a retrospective of Klee's paintings, which launched the German abstract artist into the imaginations of the populace. Starved of continental art by the war, the general public came in droves, and as John Rothenstein remembers, they 'bought the little catalogues by the thousand'. For younger artists Klee's genius for colour and idiosyncratic doodles were a 'revelation'; for detractors of modern art the exhibition was scandalous: a sign that the Tate was becoming 'indifferent to traditional values'. The new vogue for Klee was bolstered, in New York, by an exhibition at the Museum of Modern Art. With Klee's paintings still floating around the Tate (a fact which infuriated some of the lenders), and Frost being on especially friendly terms with the MoMA director, Alfred Barr, it made good commercial sense to produce a volume on the artist.

The man behind the Tate Klee retrospective was Douglas Cooper, a large man with small avian eyes, a face like 'a cottage loaf', and a dandy's dress sense. Cooper was an art lover, scholar and collector of great personal wealth, remarkable equally for his knowledge of European modern art, and his amusing effrontery. An Australian by birth, he arrived in England in 1929 and attended Cambridge where he 'became a rebel, an aesthete, and an exhibitionist who sported an Elizabethan cane dangling with pompons'.[50] He left the university of his own volition to study art, and thereafter contributed to journals such as *Horizon* and *The Burlington Magazine*. His trenchant writing on French painting drew much respect, but his withering judgements on British artists inspired fear and, sometimes, loathing. After the war he spent much of his time motoring around the continent in the wasp-coloured Rolls-Royce of his one-time lover Basil, visiting collections and exhibitions, and consorting with the likes of Picasso, Braque and Peggy Guggenheim. He would eventually settle in a colonnaded villa in the south of France, which he filled with his burgeoning collection of French Cubist and modern art.

In his brilliant memoir, *The Sorcerer's Apprentice: Picasso, Provence and Douglas Cooper*, John Richardson,

50. Richardson, *The Sorcerer's Apprentice: Picasso, Provence, and Douglas Cooper* (London: Jonathan Cape, 1983), 22.

Cooper's companion for ten years, attributes Cooper's unfortunate disposition to a set of genes inherited from his father, 'a bowler-hatted major who radiated disapproval'. As a boy, the young Cooper dangled his tiny brother over the stairwell balcony in his enormous family home; he was only persuaded from dropping the child onto the stone floor some fifty feet below by his nanny, who cautioned: 'You'll have to clean up the mess, master Douglas.' As an adult, his antisocial antics both won him acolytes and alienated those who could have been of most use to him. In her memoir, *The Duchess of Cork Street*, the art dealer Lillian Browse recalls Douglas Cooper entering her shop just as she was concluding a sale of a Bonington with some new clients: 'As the new owners were admiring their purchase, Douglas Cooper boomed out, his voice penetrating against the room's quietness: "That picture is not by Bonington." With this helpful remark to the friend he was with, he marched out of the gallery in his forceful way.' Lillian Browse shared with many the view that 'Douglas Cooper had a rare feeling for painting which, strengthened by imagination and much erudition, made him an outstanding figure in modern art. Had it not been for his general unpopularity he might well have become an inspired Director, at one time, perhaps, of the Tate.'

Much of Cooper's antagonism was directed towards England, whose institutions, parochialism and brand of snobbery he reviled. At the coronation of Queen Elizabeth II, Cooper sat amongst the cheering and animated crowd, and booed volubly as the new queen passed. For him the experience of attracting so many bewildered and angry glares was almost euphoric. His anglophobia extended to England's art, and few English artists escaped the sharp end of his pen. Of Henry Moore, he wrote: 'The imitation of weather-worn pebble and bone shapes just because nature fashioned them is not sculpture.' It was his dislike of English formulae that caused his Penguin Klee volume to break with tradition on the list of contributors of paintings. 'Let us also leave out "Esq.", a word I hate & particularly inappropriate when foreign gentlemen get nothing. I agree to "owned by".'

Cooper's association with the Klee estate began during the war when he worked sleuthing German assets and Nazi-seized artwork for the Allies. According to John Richardson, Douglas was friends with Klee's widow, Lily Klee, in Switzerland. He also was good friends with Rolf Bürgi, a wealthy Bernese businessman who owned a castle called Schlössli Belp so full of Klee's paintings you could hardly see the walls. Bürgi was a member of a circle of Swiss art lovers who were determined to prevent the Allies from seizing Klee's valuable estate, including his paintings, under the terms of the German peace agreement after the war. As Klee had carried a German passport all his life, this was no easy manoeuvre. Rolf Bürgi cunningly arranged for a 'sale': 'The more important works were deeded to a Klee *Siftung* (foundation) at the Bern Museum,' reports Richardson. 'The rest became the property of a *Gesellschaft* (corporation) under the administration of Bürgi and his friends.' Bürgi's corporation settled prices and sold work according to their own discretion, and although they did indeed save Klee for Switzerland, they also profited from the transaction considerably. Naturally, a good number of fine Klees were put aside for Cooper's collection at a reasonable cost. Strictly speaking, the set-up was dubious, but the Allied art sleuth turned a blind eye to its inconsistencies with official protocol. When Klee's son Felix was released from a Russian prisoner of war camp a few years later, claiming he had been stripped of his rightful inheritance, Cooper took the side of Bürgi and Co. As Richardson explains, 'Douglas's high principles had a way of evaporating when his interests were affected.' Cooper's connections with the Bürgi circle proved advantageous for the Tate; he loaned much of his collection to the 1945 Klee retrospective and assisted the gallery in obtaining major loans from his Bernese friends.

Peter Messer first contacted Cooper with a view to getting him to act as a liaison with the Klee estate over permissions and reproductions. Cooper, who was expert in arranging things to suit himself, roundly penned a letter to Messer in which he deftly took control of all the details of the monograph: 'I have now heard from Frau Klee and Bürgi. They are both very sympathetic to the idea of your proposed volume on Klee... I am therefore authorised by them to carry through all the negotiations on their behalf and take such decisions as may be necessary.' Cooper then set out a number of 'not very onerous' conditions that attached to the permission. These included the proviso that he would either choose the author of the monograph or write it himself, that publication would not precede the issue of a volume he had in preparation with Lund Humphries, and that he would have final and unchallengeable say in the selection of plates. Although Cooper said they issued from Lily Klee and Bürgi, there can be little doubt that Cooper moved a bit of his official weight around and devised these criteria himself.

Penguin quickly agreed to let Cooper take over the volume. The majority of the paintings came from Cooper's own collection and the collections of Bürgi and his circle in Bern. Sir Kenneth Clark only once made an attempt to guide Cooper's selection, using Peter Messer as an emissary. Cooper wrote back to Messer while holidaying in Europe: 'Many thanks for your letter... The net result of the illustrations as suggested by you has completely destroyed a fairly carefully worked out balance.' Clark made no further attempt to interfere with his arrangements.

When Frost returned from America and resumed her work on the series, she found him equally unguidable, and to her dismay, it took over two years to extract an introduction: 'Now that I am back after the perfection of Italy to the imperfection of home, I am reminded of your particular imperfection, and that is that I really must have the Klee monograph very soon. The point is, how soon?'

The eventual text was a good piece of work. 'I am glad that he has stuck to the facts,' wrote Clark to Frost. 'Most writers on Klee cannot resist the temptation of literary fancies.' Clark had only one complaint: 'If I have a fault to find, it is with the summary of German Art on page two. It is misleading to group together Menzel and Liebermann, and really they have nothing to do with Klee.' However, he asked Frost to deal discreetly with the problem herself: 'Please do not mention my name, or tell him that I have seen his introduction.' Clark was acquainted with Cooper, and was not keen to invoke his well-known wrath or malicious taunts. Fortunately, Frost's charm worked on Cooper, and the reference to Menzel was removed.

Klee was the first artist in the series who was not alive when the decision was made to produce his volume. This created a new problem: to whom should Penguin pay the £100 for the artist's fees?

Since the inception of the volume Lily Klee had died, and as Klee had carried a German passport, the £100 would be considered the assets of a German in Switzerland and subject to virtual confiscation. Therefore, 60 per cent would go to the three Allies, 20 per cent to Switzerland, and 20 per cent would be held in deposit. Bürgi wavered, first telling Frost – who knew nothing of the situation – to send the cheque to his lawyers, then asking her to forward it to Cooper. In the end, Cooper and Bürgi came clean and the £100 was returned to Penguin: 'Your Penguin book is so prominently displayed in all the bookshops of Switzerland that even the Receiver woke up,' Cooper explained. 'So here's a cheque for £100. All the more credit to Penguin's sales organisation.'

Klee appeared in the same year as *David Jones* – 1949. *The Listener* gave a favourable review:

> The Penguin series of Modern Painters continues, by dint of a carefully planned combination of good qualities, to provide the best value for money obtainable in this or, I suspect, any other country today. It is tempting to the reviewer to indulge in slight exaggerations of praise or blame: they make his review more interesting. But exaggeration is unnecessary here. On the whole, the colour plates (how rarely can this be said of the present spate of illustrated books on art and artists) are good: the proportion of an equal number of colour and half-tone plates is unusual: the artists chosen are suitable (how many good painters lose more than half their power in reduction and reproduction) and the authors who introduce them are selected with due regard to their sympathy and write with a due sense of their responsibility. The size of the page is generous enough for most purposes, and the format is modest without being flimsy. The price is surprising. Each of these items of praise sounds mild enough isolated from the rest. But taken together it is a formidable list, and the last two volumes are as good as any that have appeared.

IVON HITCHENS AND THE SUTHERLAND REPRINT

BY the 1950s *The Penguin Modern Painters* series had very little wind left in its sails, mostly as a result of economics and changing times. During the war years and immediately afterwards, England had been devoid of art books, prints and bright-coloured reproductions. According to Frost's former assistant, John Curtis, who worked at Penguin from 1953 to 1962 before becoming an art director at Weidenfeld and Nicolson, this made the Penguin series, 'an absolute revelation'. Edward Bawden's comment to his wife from Cairo – 'I look at any postcard reproduction of a painting as I would look at green fields' – was equally true in England. So welcome were the reproductions in the Penguin monographs, it was not uncommon for buyers of the series to cut them out paste them to the walls of their homes to provide a bit of cheer during the long drab days of war.

The situation in the 1950s was far removed from this. Art books proliferated – they were modern and exciting, affordable and packed with colour. *The Penguin Modern Painters* series no longer had control over a niche in the market – nor did they fulfil the moral prerogative of supporting young British artists. Despite the competition, Frost initiated numerous half-hearted attempts to revive the series. She discussed a possible monograph with the artist James Kenward; and she forwarded to Clark missives from loyal collectors of the series suggesting future monographs – on Canadian artists, Miró, Ravilious and others. It is not to be regarded as a lack of industry on Frost's part that these books were never made. As Curtis relates, 'it was typical of Penguin to get enthusiastic about projects and then drop them.' As was frequently the case, in this instance the reason was sheer economics: the books were labour intensive, expensive to produce and, given the new competition, out of vogue.

Nevertheless, in 1951, a straightforward *Henry Moore* reprint made it onto the market. In addition to these, two new English volumes were published in 1955 – a completely revised edition of *Graham Sutherland* and the monograph *Ivon Hitchens*. These books came into being mainly because they were initiated and executed outside of Frost's sphere.

The heavy gust that got *Graham Sutherland* sailing came from the notorious Douglas Cooper. In the early 1950s Sutherland was feasting on the fruits of the early patronage of Kenneth Clark and the publicity engendered by his 1944 Penguin monograph. Hans Juda's

Ambassador Editions had produced a tall, slim Sutherland volume with a text by Robert Melville, one of the best critics of the age; in 1951 Clark staged a Sutherland show at London's Institute of Contemporary Art; and in 1953 the artist had a large retrospective at the Tate. Though many critics disparaged his work, Sutherland was showered with commissions for portraits and public art and virtually became a household name. Notwithstanding the surge of interest in Sutherland, however, it is unlikely that the reprint of his volume would have proceeded if Douglas Cooper had not suggested it to Eunice Frost.

Sutherland belonged to the same café society as Cooper in the South of France, and was the only British artist Cooper did not go after with sharpened fangs, partially because, as a trustee of the Tate Gallery, he was a powerful and useful ally. In the early 1950s, Sutherland and his wife Kathy (whose fashion sense grew more and more sophisticated to keep up with Sutherland's growing reputation) were frequent guests at the villa 'Castille' of Cooper and his companion John Richardson. Sutherland used to give Cooper drawings, to which the impresario responded with jars of truffles.[51] During the height of this friendship, Eunice Frost was also developing a sort of camaraderie with Cooper, and even met him in Italy and France. Both Frost and Cooper knew Alfred Barr at the Museum of Modern Art, and Frost must have been impressed with Cooper's informal role as one of Barr's primary purchasing advisors. One can well imagine Cooper, sitting in his armchair in Castille, instructing Frost in his booming voice, 'well now, it's time for a revised edition of the Sutherland book.' Sutherland's Tate retrospective clinched the deal, since it placed a good number of the artist's pictures within convenient reach of the block-makers. In 1953, Frost informed Clark nonchalantly: 'We have decided to reprint – but in a completely revised form – Graham Sutherland's book.'

Reprinting a monograph on an artist ten years on posed difficulties. For one, Sutherland was in the midst of a transitional period in his work, including a new departure into portraiture. With recent works available at the Tate, this didn't matter as far as illustrations went, but it did make Edward Sackville-West's essay terribly out of date. Sutherland wrote to Frost:

> I spoke to Eddy Sackville-West. He didn't seem very keen [to update the text] – either a) because he thinks he doesn't understand my later work, or b) because he doesn't like it or c) because he doesn't want to write about art at all now. A letter from you to him would clear it up. You might tell him what I've told you (i.e. that I still consider his piece far the best that has ever been written on me). It might work. Otherwise we shall have to think of printing a second article (with Eddy's) by someone else.

Sackville-West ascribed more poetic reasons to his lack of ease over the matter: 'I am not – and never was – an art writer. I wrote that one essay in a fit of enthusiasm. It was, so to speak, a kind of poem – one cannot add to

51. Richardson, 112.

a poem, ten years later!' Clark washed his hands of the affair: 'I think Edward Sackville-West's article was so good for its original purpose that it ought to be reprinted, and you should find someone else to write a supplement on the later work. Alas, I have no idea who should write your supplement.'

Fortunately, it wasn't necessary to find another writer. After a good chat in the warm light of the Riviera, with cocktails and plenty of recent pictures in hand, Sutherland talked Sackville-West into reconsidering his decision. 'I have allowed myself to be persuaded – very dubiously, I must confess – into revising the article, and enlarging it to include comment on the pictures of the post-war period.'

Sutherland's happy gloating over his handling of Sackville-West came to an abrupt halt when the new text appeared. He resented Sackville-West's treatment of his recent portraiture; he also dismissed as nonsensical the author's claims to have found a face, formed by Christ's nipples, rib-shadow and abdomen, in the painting *Crucifixion*. Scenting Sutherland's disapproval, Sackville-West in turn went on the defensive: 'It is [Sutherland's] own fault for insisting that I do something I no longer feel able to do adequately,' he complained in a letter to Frost. Frost, claiming that length was the main issue, diplomatically suggested some calculated pruning. She could report to Sutherland a few weeks later: 'I am delighted that he took my suggestions so well. He has cut from the paragraph "Sutherland's portraits are not obliging, nor are they necessarily exhaustive..." That then leaves him to go on with the general comment, "Nevertheless, I should be surprised if portraiture were ever to become more than a sideline".' In the end, Sutherland's monograph contained only one portrait: that of Lord Beaverbrook, a Canadian-born newspaper proprietor, wartime Cabinet Minister and brilliant amateur historian.

Knowing that Frost was concurrently working on volumes on Braque and Picasso, and that following Cooper's advice, these were to appear, for the first time, in a portrait format, Sutherland was keen that his monograph also took the revised shape. Kenneth Clark recoiled from the idea: 'Personally I think it would be a great pity to change the landscape form... The old series created a quantity of goodwill, and I think that a lot of this would be lost if the physical shape of the series were to be altered.' Frost then consulted with Cooper, who sided with Sutherland. 'I am delighted about your decision with regard to the altered shape,' the artist wrote to Frost. 'Also – that Douglas doesn't mind.'

Sutherland's most articulate detractor, the St Ives artist, Patrick Heron, happened to be Ivon Hitchens' most robust admirer, and consequently the author of Ivon Hitchens, which appeared at the same time as the *Graham Sutherland* reprint. The spark behind the monograph was John Curtis, a personal friend of Patrick Heron, who remembers: 'Heron was very keen on Ivon Hitchens. Hitchens should really have appeared with the earlier *Modern Painters*, but I suggested the idea to Frost and she said "Okay, you produce Patrick Heron". I was surprised when it went through. I remember going to look at blocks with Hitchens.'

It is hardly surprising that Heron praised Hitchens to the sky while deriding Sutherland's work. Heron's own painting had been compared with Hitchens before he had even become aware of the artist. They were both colourists, influenced by the Fauves, and both owed their handling of paint to a preoccupation with the 'pictorial' aspect of painting, as opposed to its literary, or atmospheric, aspect. Heron was obsessed with the way in which colour creates space, not with how paintings reflect or evoke the real world, and he had become an avid proselytiser on the subject. His first regular stint as an art writer, at *The New Statesman*, lasted until the literary editor decided that the paper's readers deserved 'at least some respite' from 'abstruse' ruminations, 'week after week', on space in painting.[52]

Heron first established himself as Ivon Hitchens' cheerleader when he reviewed an exhibition at the Leicester Galleries in June 1952. A modified version of this short essay appeared in his book *The Changing Forms of Art*, 1955. In both articles Heron blamed the British public's taste and sensibilities for Hitchens' self-imposed reclusiveness:

In a country where painting is understood primarily in terms of literature, if at all; where critics still react first and foremost to what they call the 'mood' or 'atmosphere' of a painting, instead of its pictorial qualities, its palpable reality; *and*, therefore, where realism's opposite, pure non-figurative abstraction, is also very acceptable – a painter in whom all the virtues of the central tradition in Western painting are so strong is bound to appear lonely.

When Heron submitted his text for the Penguin monograph, he resumed his diatribe against the aesthetic mindset of the English in the very first paragraph; he also slipped in an attack against Ben Nicholson and Sutherland. Frost, who was keeping watch, cautioned him to modify his attack. Heron then made a few dilatory attempts at manoeuvering Frost into a position of consent:

Please forgive me for keeping you waiting. I was not merely lolling in the sun indifferent to necessity (though I am sitting sunbathing in this rocky garden as I write now!). I had to go away from here for a week to take a summer school of painting single handed, in Wiltshire, for a week:
1) I still feel the first paragraph might remain. It seems to me that it is not at all an attack upon the reader who has the book in his hands but rather a criticism of 'we English' – to which the sympathetic reader will say (I hope) 'Hear! Hear! Quite right!' What the unsympathetic reader thinks doesn't matter, I think. Or rather – we must not adjust our efforts to his incomprehension! We must calculate on his eavesdropping, as it were. The truth about the English attitude to painting cannot be too much emphasised: i.e. we are, as a nation (even when educated) quite blind to visual things. Hitchens stands for vision – in the physical, sensuous, actual sense. Hence my opening, with its pillorying of the blind, the intellectually

52. Mel Gooding, introduction to *Painter as Critic: Patrick Heron: Selected Writing* (London: Tate Gallery, 1998), viii.

genteel and inoffensive.
2) I have capitulated about the inclusion of the names of Ben and G.S. Those who are with me will have a pretty fair idea to whom I refer (in my revised version) while those who aren't (and who might take offence) will not, I think, recognise the unnamed exemplars.

Inevitably, Frost turned him around with reason and diplomacy. He agreed to cut out the more 'acid' sentences, in the opening paragraph, and switch it with the gentler second paragraph. It is a tribute to Frost's tact that he felt indebted to her rather than compromised: 'Many thanks for your last letter. And for so patiently coaching me in the art of flighting one's darts silently!'

★

Although *Braque* was published in 1959, it was with the publication of *Ivon Hitchens* in November 1955 that the role of *The Penguin Modern Painters* as an emissary of new British modern artists came to a final halt. It had established the careers of artists such as Ben Nicholson, Victor Pasmore and David Jones, and it had provided a colourful tonic and morale-booster during the war. But its form and function were outdated and its editor tired. As early as 1951, Sir Kenneth Clark replied to a collector of the series: 'I ceased to edit the Penguin books some years ago and do not know if they are contemplating adding to the series. I know that they found that delays in production were very troublesome and with present-day cost of production, I think it possible that they will not be able to keep the series on.' The next year, he declined an invitation from Lane to attend a cocktail party for a group photograph of Penguin editors. Then in 1954, he wrote to Frost, as he had many times before: 'You have done all the work during the last ten years, and it is high time your name appeared and you got credit for it.'

John Curtis attributes the demise of the series in part to the declining health of Eunice Frost, in part to Penguin attitudes in general in the 1950s:

The thing about Eunice was that she was not very easy. She was going through a period of ill-health – some days she wouldn't come in. She was loyal to staff, but difficult. She felt passionately about things. She was mostly doing fiction. The list suffered – if you look at the Penguin lists, it goes through a bad period until the arrival of Tony Godwin. The reason for this was that Penguin had a monopoly and thought they were an institution when they took off – they could say and do what they wanted. In the 1950s, after the war, other paperback houses started up.

In 1960, in ill-health, Frost was forced to retire from the company that had been the focus of her entire life. Her role was taken over in part by Godwin, who heralded a brave new age for Penguin. Despite his magic touch, however, it seemed that the success of future slim art monographs on young contemporary artists at Penguin was tainted with an unshakeable curse.

In the 1970s Penguin tried to revive the idea with a series called *Penguin New Art*, but only four of a projected sixteen volumes were ever published, with

Richard Morphet as advisory editor. These were on Patrick Caulfield by Christopher Finch, Robyn Denny by David Thompson, Frank Stella by Robert Rosenblum; Claes Oldenburg by Ellen H. Johnson. The series was indeed slick, but it lacked the friendly, householdy charm charm of its predecessor. No doubt, Frank Stella's parallel lines, Robyn Denny's geometric forms – often resembling details of Greek borders – Patrick Caulfield's interiors, scenes of the bay and still-lifes – all so stylised they lack the detail even of cartoons – and Claes Oldenburg's soft bathtubs and giant ice-cream cones, posed a greater mystery to the general public than Paul Nash's Surrealist paintings had in the 1940s. The series definitely hadn't enough appeal for a mass audience. It remains a curious note in the history of Penguin and art-book publishing, that while each of the first four volumes of *The Penguin Modern Painters* in 1944 sold in excess of 40,000, *Penguin New Art* volumes could not command sales of 3,000.

The fact that the series fizzled out in the 1950s in no way diminishes Eunice Frost's achievement, the series' importance as wartime tonic, or the impact it had on the lives of the young, under-acknowledged artists who were the lucky subjects of monographs. The esteem with which these artists and those who wrote on them held Frost could be seen in 1956, when she was invited to receive the OBE for her contribution to British publishing. The letters poured in, and amongst them, were kind congratulations from people like Ivon Hitchens.

BRAQUE: THE BITTER END

IN June 1953 Frost had written to Clark: 'Would you support the idea of adding Braque to the *Penguin Modern Painters*? We ourselves would like this very much and I have talked it over with Bill Williams, in case you would like to have a word with him.' Holbein-Verlag was doing a large Braque folio and it seemed to Frost a good opportunity to get photographers to work on plates for a Penguin monograph at the same time.

For all his admiration of Braque's paintings, Clark resisted the proposal, and felt that Braque was too well established: 'Your series was begun to introduce more or less unknown painters.' Clark mellowed after seeing Richardson's Braque proposal, which he praised as being 'both representative and economical', but despite his initial support of Klee, he never quite reconciled himself to what Frost described as 'the new series'. And when Frost added Picasso, Rouault, Gettuso, Francis Bacon, and Ivon Hitchens to the new list, he showed a shocking lack of foresight: 'Whether there is really any point in introducing the people of South Shields at this late hour to Matisse and Picasso I am far from certain. It seems to me that these painters were the product of a highly sophisticated society and can never be genuinely popular, although people may buy them out of snobbishness and curiosity.' He concluded by attempting to draw a final line under his involvement in the series. Frost replied: 'Please have no more fear that we are intending to go commercially after Renoir, and the others, for the sake of South Shields... We hope, though, that you will allow your name to be associated with, and appear on, the six more Modern Painters we would like to do – and with which we seemed in sympathy.'

While the vocal Marxist art critic, John Berger, was to write the Gettuso, and his contemporary David Sylvester was to produce the Bacon monograph, Frost was most eager for Douglas Cooper to write the book on Picasso. That way Braque and Picasso, the two great Cubists would appear as a set, and since they invariably featured in the same collections, the photographers could make the plates at the same time.

Within months, John Richardson had managed to make impressive inroads into the Braque volume, and Kenneth Clark had even agreed to put his name on it as editor. One obstacle, however, remained. So ill had Braque been, no one had asked him for permission to produce a book of his work. 'Braque has had an operation for appendicitis (so-called),' Richardson wrote to Frost: 'This has been kept rather quiet, for the poor man already had 'everything out' during the war, and it was thought that people might jump to obvious conclusions, rightly or wrongly, as to the seriousness of his illness if the news was broadcast.' In December 1953, Douglas Cooper went to Paris hoping to meet the artist, but he was still recuperating at his house in Normandy. Weeks later, Braque was still in no state to answer letters or take decisions. 'If you have heard nothing from me, it is not my fault,' wrote Richardson in January 1954. 'Braque has been fearfully ill with prostate trouble. Now at last he is better.'

In April, Frost took a tour through Europe, which included lunch with Peggy Guggenheim, a stop-over in Milan, and finally, a stay at Castille. Cooper and Richardson knew how to entertain, and characteristically Frost was taken about to visit members of their circle. One such individual was Dora Maar, Picasso's mistress before Françoise. According to John Richardson, Dora Maar developed the theory that when the woman in Picasso's life changed, everything changed: 'The style that epitomised the new companion, the house or apartment they shared, the poet who served as a supplementary muse, the *tertulia* (group of friends) that provided the understanding and support he craved, and the dog that rarely left his side.' Frost lunched with Maar in a fortified seventeenth-century house on the top of a hilltop village called Ménerbes, not far from Richardson and Cooper. The house belonged to the Russian artist, Nicolas de Staël, renowned for his minimalist landscapes, and an avid disciple of Braque. At the very least, Frost's lunch must have been a pleasant affair; as Richardson remembers, 'Staël had been elected to the Czar's College of Pages at the age of two'; his courtesy and charm were impeccable.

Between lunches and bullfights at Arles, and trips to Montpellier, Frost set aside business-like afternoons to work with Richardson on the Braque. Arguably, no one but Richardson could have had the contacts or wherewithal to put together a better or more representative selection of the Cubist's work. Where Cooper's métier was Picasso, early in his career Richardson made Braque his special concern. In some senses, Cooper and Picasso, both overbearing, needy and eccentric personalities, were well-matched. Richardson, who suffered deeply, but silently from his mentor's cantankerous nature, may well have identified with Braque who, likewise, shouldered Picasso's heavy demands of friendship and maintained an aura of quiet self-sufficiency. Braque 'was the antithesis of Picasso', wrote Richardson, 'cool, meditative, at peace'. Richardson spent long hours conversing with Braque in his studio; and the young critic lined his own study with some of the artist's finest paintings. 'On my first visit to the artist's studio,' Richardson remembers, 'I felt I had arrived at the very heart of painting.'

In the summer of 1956, John and Douglas spent the summer at Cooper's London home at Egerton Terrace. Frost met them for a saddle of lamb and a conversation full of Cooper's lively, if derogatory, humour. Frost came up with a plan to get Braque and Picasso to draw original covers for the books, and provided Cooper and Richardson with paper and specifications to give the artists. Departing from the earlier volumes, the books would be portrait format, though the same size.

Meanwhile, Frost desperately needed the texts if she was to attain her objective of publishing the two books the following year. Months later, when Cooper and Richardson had returned to Castille, she abandoned her good humour to reveal a growing sense of frustration: 'You have put me off so often that our Production Department is disinclined to listen any more when I plead for any action on Braque and Picasso. Surely you can see that it is only in your interests that I keep repeating repeating [sic] my demands that you disgorge your texts.'

Some of the delay may have been due to Cooper and Richardson's fast-track lifestyle. Castille was the destination of endless droves of guests: Picasso and his ex-lovers, Braque, Cocteau, Graham Sutherland, the Queen Mother, and the publisher George Weidenfeld to name but a few. It also contained one of the most valuable collections of Cubist art in the country, and attracted dealers and collectors and curiosity-seekers in swarms. When Cooper wasn't receiving – or turning away – the rich and famous, he was organising international art exhibitions. However, it was sometimes the more ordinary guests that did the most damage. As Richardson complained to Frost: 'Douglas's parents have been here for a fortnight, and they need entertaining 24 hours a day: they flourish, we don't – and all too little work is getting done.'

In the early months of 1957, Richardson's introduction finally arrived – messy, annotated, and badly in need of retyping – but a final text nonetheless: 'I have incorporated virtually all the suggestions that you made,' he wrote to Frost, 'also disadvantageous comparisons with Picasso and lengthy discussions of pictures not reproduced have nearly all been removed. The only thing I have not done is to shorten the beginning which both Douglas and Anthony Blunt feel should remain as it is. If you feel strongly about this, however, I can always do a bit more surgery.'

The essay Richardson wrote was detailed, comprehensive and, in the spirit of many first-time writers, interminable. Richardson's academic style revealed little of the remarkable wit and clarity of his later writing, but nonetheless displayed the artistic sensitivity and erudition which would settle his career. His introduction for the 1961 *Braque*, a folio published by the Oldbourne Press, would be a good deal better. And despite his early penchant for Braque, in the end it was him, not Cooper, who would chart Picasso's life in a massive three-volume biography.

A month later Braque's drawing for the cover arrived featuring one of his famous birds flying towards its nest. For Richardson, the design was a particularly meaningful. Both Braque and Richardson used to visit a vast bird reserve known as La Tour du Valat, established by their mutual friend, the ornithologist Lukas Hoffman. As Richardson would recall in *The Sorcerer's Apprentice:*

Braque told me how the apparition of a heron flying low above the marshes had inspired his large 1955 *Bird Returning to Its Nest*, of all the late paintings the one that meant the most to him. Maybe because I shared his feelings for the Camargue, Braque gave me an oil study for this haunting work. I remember him saying how, on still, gray days, the sky seemed to reflect the lagoons rather than the other way round, and the birds seemed to swim through the air.

Hans Schmoller spent months trying to get Braque's sketch to fit the cover, and much time was lost corresponding with Richardson about its format. 'Braque is too old, too ill and too grand to order around,' Richardson wrote apologetically, 'so I daren't ask him to alter his design.' In the end, it was Richardson who found a solution: 'Use a reversed duplicate of the bird to fill in the black space to the right of the sketch, and type *The Penguin Modern Painters* along the bottom of the cover.'

As an author, Richardson had proved himself slow, but conscientious and, importantly, amenable to suggestions. Working with Cooper was a less healthy collaboration. Frost and her successors would spend years trying to drag a text from him. And Penguin spent a small fortune on plates and reproductions. 'Picasso has become an immediate reality,' Cooper assured Frost in 1956:

If my mind could turn over at the moment, it would be doing so around Picasso – BUT I have been travelling for eight weeks, I have done three major exhibitions, made speeches and lectures in three different languages, driven 6,000 km. – and am now snoozling half in & half out of bed, pending departure for New York on 25 November for 6 weeks. HELL! I am also organising a big show of Braque for Edinburgh Festival & London in August – October 1957.

When Cooper was in London in 1957, Frost wrote, with her usual good humour: 'I shall attach myself like a suffragette to your railings until I get that Picasso text out of you.' However, the situation remained much the same seven years later, after Frost had retired and Tony Godwin had taken over plans for the monograph.

As Cooper wrote many books on art, it is hard to say why he had such difficulty producing a short essay on Picasso. One reason may well have been that he was afraid of comparison with his young ward, Richardson, in the way that a master might fear being outshone by his apprentice. Another reason is that he may have found it impossible to achieve the high standards he set himself: 'I am indeed taking a lot of trouble to try and write a sensible basic manual for appreciating Picasso in language which schoolboys can understand,' Cooper wrote in 1963. 'This is not easy – that's why it takes so long. In fact I have to do several versions of the text to get what I want, and to say something different from others – but I plod on – I've been ill.'

The reason for Cooper's prevarications may have been that the monograph came to symbolise a disagreeable period in his life. Shortly after Richardson completed his Braque monograph, he made his first attempt to break with his difficult and cantankerous partner, to start a life on his own terms. He left for New York shortly before Christmas 1958 amid a torrent of threats and abusive farewells. When he returned, several months later, Cooper was on his best behaviour. It was December 1960 before Richardson left definitively, but even at the end of 1958, the ten-year companionship was as good as over. As Richardson explains in his memoir: 'The prospect of spending most of the rest of my life as a resentful apprentice to a capricious sorcerer had little appeal for me.' Since *Braque* and *Picasso* were meant originally to be twin volumes, working on the text must have been a bitter task for the eccentric collector. Especially when Frost, who knew nothing of the impending break-up, wrote in March 1959, 'I warn you I am going to pest and pester, from now on, about that Picasso text... And incidentally what did you think of John's Braque about which I never heard a word? I only hope this doesn't signify disappointment.'

A general report was circulated within Penguin in 1961 with respect to the Douglas Cooper situation. Almost £2,000 had been paid out on photographs of paintings, reproduction fees, blockmaking, proofing, retouching, and reproofing. No contract could be found, so it was agreed that Cooper had never been tied down to any particular date for producing his text. Some information about the backdrop to the Picasso monograph was provided:

> The original suggestion seems to have been for a book illustrated by Picasso on *Buffon's Natural History*, and from 1949 onwards the correspondence consists mainly of a discussion as to who owned the rights in the illustrations: it was finally decided that Picasso did. AL said Douglas Cooper could offer Picasso £250 for the right to reproduce illustrations in a *King Penguin*, but it is not clear whether this was the Buffon or an idea which seems to have come up later for a *King Penguin* of Picasso portraits. By 1954 plans for both a *King Penguin* portraits and the *Modern Painters* volume seemed to be under way and Miss Frost was writing off for permissions to reproduce and arranging for photographers to make colour plates of the pictures we wish to use in the *Modern Painters* volume. By the end of 1955 the idea of the *King Penguin* portraits seems to have been dropped.

The general report concluded with 1959, at which point, it was reported that 'both [Cooper] and [Frost] were very keen for the book to appear in the Penguin Festival [i.e. the 25th Anniversary in 1960].'

With £2,000 already invested in the Picasso book, it was difficult for editors at Penguin to know how whether to drop the project or re-commission the text. They opted for the latter course and paid Cooper £300 to produce the introduction by March 1963. Two months after the deadline, Cooper wrote promising he would have the text ready for August: 'Your text is all I think about, by day & by night... Now it's up to you, because the book will be written anyway, even if you don't want to be its publishers.' In August Godwin wrote encouragingly: 'The weather here in England this summer has been absolutely dreadful and the receipt of your manuscript on Picasso would be something to mitigate the really rather barren summer.' When, in March 1964, the text still had not arrived, Godwin decided to apply a heavy hand: 'There comes a point when further forbearance becomes suicide. Under the terms of our contract we are free now to re-commission this book using the existing illustrations with someone such as Roland Penrose. I shall go ahead with this unless you deliver the text to us by June 1st 1964.'

The letter elicited a bilious response from Cooper, reproduced here, almost in its entirety:

Your letter has arrived at a moment when I am actually sitting with my desk covered with sheets of typescript and MS of the book in question. I have been at work on it seriously for the last few weeks again and am doing nothing else. It will be finished as soon as I have written just exactly what I want to write. I am not going to tie myself down to a fixed date because I don't at this minute know how fast I am going to continue getting the MS into final shape. I know you won't believe that this is true, but I will put it on record none the less because if you were here you would see that it is actually the case. You have the advantage of a regiment of secretaries at your disposal to take dictation and type...

If you wish to 'recommission' a text on Picasso from another author in place of the book I am writing the responsibility for and consequences of doing so will fall entirely on the firm of Penguin... But when you talk of 'using the existing illustrations' to accompany the text of another author than myself you should realise that it will not be legally possible to do so without my consent and co-operation. I will give you two reasons for this:

1) ...it is recognised that the cover design is my personal property and can ONLY be used for a book written by myself unless I give 'express written permission'.

2) four of the illustrations in question are of paintings which are in my possession. It would be an infringement of legal rights for you to reproduce these in a book without my written consent.

I was interested to learn from another London publisher the other day that you had offered him an option on producing a hard-cover edition of my future book.

Before you feel too suicidal, let me tell you that I was talking the other day with a publisher in New York, who showed me the material for a book which was commissioned twelve years ago, for which there is still no text, and in which $15,000 has already been invested.

If I am correctly informed, the name of your other business enterprise is Better Books. Your letter would scarcely suggest that you are trying to live up to the principle.

Astonishingly, Godwin extended Cooper's deadline again, this time until March 1965. Cooper's subsequent behaviour was telling: when upon wandering into Hans Schmoller's office, he discovered the Picasso drawing for the cover hanging on the wall – framed and behind glass – he demanded the picture back in a state of pique. Later he would relate the story with mock horror and indignation: 'I went into Penguin and I saw my Picasso.'

The text never appeared. 'In your last letter to me you wrote that 'unless we receive the complete manuscript from you by March 1st 1965 our agreement with you will be at an end,' Cooper instructed after the final deadline. 'You have not received the manuscript and therefore I consider that no further contract exists between us. This will no doubt be a relief to you as it brings to an end a chapter of muddling incompetence on the part of Penguin such as one does not often meet with among publishers.'

★

It takes no genius to see that Cooper's accusations were absurd, and that he had merely, in his precocious way, taken Penguin for a ride.

The history of *The Penguin Modern Painters* series is a story of the highest competence during a time of war, economic deprivation and great personal sacrifice. It is the story of a handful of people's commitment to the cause of keeping British art alive and enlivening the cultural life of the masses. Even if the Picasso monograph had been published, it would hardly have stood comfortably alongside along a series featuring Ben Nicholson's brave attempts to procure a British abstract tradition, Paul Nash's marvellous propensity for finding beauty in the plane wreckage on the coast of England, and Betjeman's friendly assertions of John Piper's 'Englishness'. The American volumes, or the one on Portinari, did indeed make proud additions to the series. But, the series remained, at its core, British. Cooper's letter was the swan-song of the series, not least because it showed how much had changed. What remains so special about *The Penguin Modern Painters* series is the legacy of goodwill, humour, and spirited co-operation amongst friends (and rivals) that helped establish it at its outset. Once this was gone, the series fizzled out. It is to the importance of goodwill in all ventures that this book provides some testimony.

APPENDICES

THE PENGUIN MODERN PAINTERS
A CHECKLIST

MP1 Henry Moore *by Geoffrey Grigson*
published: April 1944 (1943 on title-page verso)
white and cream cover

reprint: November 1944
do: June 1946; photograph of artist (p.6); text still begins as 1944: 'Henry Moore is now 44 years old'
do: 1951; cover grey-blue; no photograph; text now begins 'Henry Moore is now 53 years old'

MP2 Graham Sutherland *by Edward Sackville-West*
published: April 1944 (1943 on title-page verso)
white and cream cover

reprint: November 1945
second edition, 1955; with many new plates;
vertical format; blue-grey cover; d/w with colour reproduction of *Palm and House* (Plate 1)
(variant) d/w front flap printed $1.75, with 7/6 sticker superimposed

MP3 Duncan Grant *by Raymond Mortimer*
published: April 1944
white and cream cover

reprint: October 1945
reprint: 1948; brown cover, in heavier card

MP4 Paul Nash *by Herbert Read*
published: April 1944
white and cream cover
reprint: October 1944
revised reprint: 1948; brown cover
do: blue-grey cover; d/w with colour reproduction of *Equivalents for the Megaliths* (Plate 17)

MP5 Matthew Smith *by Philip Hendy*
published: December 1944
white and cream cover

MP6 John Piper *by John Betjeman*
published: December 1944
white and cream cover
reprint: 1948; brown cover, in heavier card

MP7 Edward Burra *by John Rothenstein*
published: December 1945
white and cream cover

MP8 Victor Pasmore *by Clive Bell*
published: December 1945
white and cream cover

MP9 Edward Bawden *by J.M. Richards*
published: November 1947 (1946 on title-page verso)
brown cover; d/w with colour reproduction of *Cattle Market, Braintree* (Plate 29)

MP10 Stanley Spencer *by Eric Newton*
published: September 1947
brown cover; d/w with colour reproduction of *The Last Supper* (Plate 5)
fount: Monotype Lutetia (the only volume which identifies the typeface)

MP11 Ben Shahn *by James Thrall Soby*
published: September 1947
green cover (the only example in the series); d/w with colour reproduction of *Girl Jumping Rope* (Plate 19)
(variants): black panel on cover; copies with 'The Museum of Modern Art, New York', above 'Penguin Books' on title-page; copies with correction slip pasted in; copies with d/w printed 'one dollar'

MP12 William Nicholson *by Robert Nichols*
published: December 1948
brown cover; d/w with colour reproduction of *Mushrooms* (Plate 21)
reissue: blue-grey cover
(variant): 'Price in Australia 5/6' sticker

MP13 Ben Nicholson *by John Summerson*
published: August 1948
brown cover (heavier card); d/w with colour reproduction of *Painted Relief* (Plate 1)
(variant): as MP12

MP14 Frances Hodgkins *by Myfanwy Evans*
published: December 1948
brown cover; d/w with colour reproduction of *Wings on Water* (Plate 11)
reissue: blue-grey cover, with d/w as above

MP15 David Jones *by Robin Ironside*
published: April 1949
blue-grey cover; d/w – not seen
reissue: d/w now priced 5/- instead of original 3/6

MP16 Paul Klee *by Douglas Cooper*
published: July 1949
blue-grey cover; d/w with colour reproduction of *Houses by the Sea* (Plate 1). (Only seen on 1953 rpt.)
reprint: 1950
do: 1952
do: 1953

MP17 Ivon Hitchens *by Patrick Heron*
published: November 1955
blue-grey cover; d/w with colour reproduction of *Waterfall, Terwick Mill* (Plate 3)
originally announced as **Edward Ardizzone** *by V.S. Pritchett*

MP18 not issued
originally announced as **Pedro Figari** *by C. Denby Miller*
also mooted as **Pablo Picasso** *by Douglas Cooper*

MP19 Edward Hopper *by Lloyd Goodrich*
published: February 1950 (1949 on title-page verso)
blue-grey cover; d/w – not seen

MP20 Georges Braque *by John Richardson*
published: January 1959
size: 177mm x 223 mm; vertical format
cover: original design, incorporating artist's name and illustration (not among plates included); d/w repeats cover
text: runs to 32 pp.
printer: Tillotsons (Bolton) Ltd.

BRAZILIAN EDITION

Portinari by Lelio Landucci
published: 1947
Arte no Brasil: Ediçoes Pinguim (numbered 1 inside)
larger format, 232 mm x 200 mm, landscape
light blue cover
16 pp. text (in two columns), 32 pp. plates, alternate colour and black-and-white
printer: Tipografia Mercantil, Quitands, 47
colour plates: Latt & Cia, Lavradio, 168
publisher: Editôra Penguin Limitada, Avenida Churchill 109, Rio de Janeiro, Brasil
price: PREÇO CR$ 30,00 on rear cover

This checklist is based on that provided in *PC35* by David Hall, who has supplied additional information for this revision. The help of Chris Barling, Don Dale-Jones, Steve Hare, Brian Kesterton, Colin Laker, Hannah Lowery, Karin Mango, Donald Muir, Judith Neal, Elizabeth Paton, Joe Pearson, Bryan Platt, Tanya Schmoller, Tony Skelton, Roy Turner, Michael Walsh and Stephen Wycherley is also gratefully acknowledged.

Russell Edwards

A NOTE ON DESIGN

Although virtually every title in *The Penguin Modern Painters* differs, sometimes in minor detail, from every other, the bulk of the issues were produced in one of two main styles. There are some (near-) constants. The volumes are in landscape format, except for the last issues, MP2 (second edition) and MP20. The size remains the same, 223 mm x 177mm in landscape, and its equivalent in vertical format. In general, there are twelve pages of text (more in MP20) and 32 pages of plates, arranged alternately in colour and black-and-white (but somewhat differently in the second edition of MP2). The editor throughout was Sir Kenneth Clark (although he is not listed in the last two issues), and Alfred H. Barr, Jr., is associated as American Editor for MP11 and MP19.

Style1 covers the earliest publications, from the launch of the series in 1944 to 1947, i.e. MP1 to MP8. The most obvious evidence of the style is the cover, divided into equal horizontal bands of white and cream, printed in capitals with the name of the subject prominent in the centre. A 'laughing penguin' device, facing right, graces the cover. Art paper is used throughout, for both plates and text, and the text pages use red rules. The wartime issues of 1944-5 (i.e. MP1 to MP8) were stapled, and had no spines, but the reprints of MP1 to MP4 which appeared after the war were sewn, and had free endpapers and a blank spine.

The **printers** were:
Hunt, Barnard & Co. Ltd ., The Sign of the Dolphin, London & Aylesbury, Buckinghamshire (MP1 to MP6)
John Swain & Son, Ltd., Noel Street, London W.1 and Barnet (MP 7, MP8)
The **colour plates** were produced by:
John Swain (MP1, MP4 to MP6)
W.F. Sedgwick, Ltd. (MP2, MP3, MP7, MP8)

A distinct change in appearance comes with the issues of 1947 and after, when the series had gained its second breath. The most obvious feature of **Style 2**, which includes MP9 through to M19 and reprints during that period, is the card cover in a single overall colour – brown (MP9, MP10, MP12 to MP14), green (MP11), or blue-grey (MP15 to MP17, MP19 and MP2 [second edition]). The series title on the cover is now printed in italic. All these volumes have free endpapers. The earlier ones (MP9 to MP11) remain sewn, with a blank spine; the later ones are perfect bound and have the title printed on the spine. From MP10 onwards non-art paper is used for the text pages, and the red rules and the artist's photograph on page 6 are dropped. The free-standing 'laughing penguin' device remains on MP9 to MP11, and is enclosed in a roundel on MP12, MP13 and MP15. A more refined Tschichold penguin roundel, facing left, is used on MP14, MP16 and all subsequent issues.

The **printers** were:
The Baynard Press, London (MP9, MP11, MP12, MP14, MP15, MP19)
Silk & Terry Ltd., Birmingham (MP10, MP13)
Hazell, Watson & Viney, Ltd., Aylesbury & London (MP16)
Hunt, Barnard & Co. Ltd., Aylesbury, Bucks. (MP17)

Colour plates were by:
John Swain & Son (MP9 to MP13, MP17), who also printed the plates made by:
W.F. Sedgwick, Ltd., London (MP14, MP15)
The Sun Engraving Co. Ltd., Watford, Herts. (MP16)

A further significant development was the decision to issue from 1948 new titles and reprints in dust-wrappers, bearing a reproduction of one of the colour plates; this might be said to constitute a **Style 3,** although under the wrappers the volumes were in Style 2 format.

By the time of the last two issues, the second edition of MP2 (1955) and MP20 (1959), the series was clearly languishing but, although those two titles are considerably different in form from each other, they share a new vertical format which may have been seen as the pattern for the future, a **Style 4** for a remarkable venture.

A NOTE ON PRICES

The earliest issues were priced at two shillings and sixpence (2/6), and that information is printed on the inside front cover of MP5 to MP7 (1944-5). By 1947 the price had risen to three shillings and sixpence (3/6), as printed on the rear cover of MP9 and subsequent titles. That price was held for many years – a 1963 stocklist shows four old titles (MP9, M10, MP12, MP13) still available at that price – but from 1955 new issues and reprints increased in price. In the latter case, the adjustment could be made by issuing the volumes in a price-adjusted dustwrapper, as happened when the price of MP14 and MP15, originally published at 3/6, was increased to five shillings (5/-). MP17 and the second edition of MP2 were published at 7/6, and the last title, MP20 at 8/6 in 1959.

SELECT BIBLIOGRAPHY

Allen, Christopher. *Art in Australia From Colonization to Postmodernism*. London: Thames and Hudson, 1947.

The Arts in War Time: A Report on the Work of the C.E.M.A., 1942 and 1943. London, 1944.

Barty-King, Hugh. *Her Majesty's Stationery Office, The Story of the First 200 Years. 1786-1986*. Her Majesty's Stationery Office, 1986.

Berthoud, Roger. *Graham Sutherland: A Biography*. London: Faber and Faber, 1982.

Berthoud, Roger. *The Life of Henry Moore*. London: Faber and Faber, 1987.

Bliss, Douglas Percy. *Edward Bawden*. Godalming, Surrey: The Pendomer Press, 1980.

Browse, Lillian. *Duchess of Cork Street, the Autobiography of an Art Dealer*. London: Giles de la Mare, 1999.

Burke, Joseph. *The Paintings of Russell Drysdale*. Sydney: Ure Smith, 1951.

Checkland, Sarah Jane. *Ben Nicholson: The Vicious Circles of his Life and Art*. London: John Murray, 2000.

Clark, Kenneth. *Another Part of the Wood: A Self-portrait*. London: Murray, 1974.

Clark, Kenneth. *The Other Half: A Self-portrait*. London: Murray, 1977.

Corbett, Val. *Helen Sutherland at Cockley Moor, 1939-1965*. Penrith: Midnight Oil, 1996.

Dutton, Geoffrey. *Russell Drysdale*. London: Thames and Hudson, 1964.

Eates, Margot. *Paul Nash, The Master of the Image, 1889-1946*. London: John Murray, 1973.

Gardiner, Margaret. 'A Portrait of Ben Nicholson', *Modern Painters 2*, no. 3 (autumn, 1989).

Goodway, David, ed., *Herbert Read Reassessed*. Liverpool: Liverpool University Press, 1998.

Hare, Steve. *Penguin Portrait: Allen Lane and the Penguin Editors, 1935-1970*. London: Penguin, 1995.

Heron, Patrick. *Painter as Critic: Patrick Heron: Selected Writing*. Introduction by Mel Gooding. London: Tate Gallery, 1998.

Hodgkins, Frances. *Letters of Frances Hodgkins*. Edited by Linda Gill. Auckland: Auckland University Press, 1993.

Hoggart, Richard, Sir Robert Lusty, and Harry Paroissien. *Tributes to Allen Lane at a Service of Thanksgiving for his Life and Work, 1902-1970*. Addresses given at St Martin-in-the-Fields on 18 August 1970. Cambridge: Privately Printed, 1970.

Holman, Valerie. 'Art Books Against the Odds: Phaidon in England 1938-1950', *Visual Resources* 15, no. 3 (1999).

Howell, Arthur. *Frances Hodgkins, Four Vital Years*. Foreword by John Piper. London: Rockcliff, 1951.

Ingrams, Richard, and Piper, John. *Piper's Places, John Piper in England and Wales.* London: Chatto and Windus, Hogarth Press, 1983.

Kent, Rockwell. Introduction. *Portinari, His Life and Art.* Chicago: University of Chicago Press, 1940.

King, James. *The Last Modern, A Life of Herbert Read.* London: Weidenfeld and Nicolson, 1990.

Khoroche, Peter. *Ivon Hitchens.* London: André Deutsch, 1990.

Lynton, Norbert. *Ben Nicholson.* London: Phaidon, 1993.

McCormick, E.H. *Portrait of Frances Hodgkins.* Auckland: Auckland University Press, 1981.

McLaine, Ian. *Ministry of Morale: Home Front Morale and the Ministry of Information in World War II.* London: George Allen and Unwin, 1979.

McLean, Ruari. *Jan Tschichold: Typographer.* London: Lund Humphries, 1990.

Meyers, Jeffrey. *The Enemy: A Biography of Wyndham Lewis.* London: Routledge and Kegan Paul, 1980.

Morpurgo, J.E. *Allen Lane, King Penguin: A Biography.* London: Hutchinson of London, 1979.

Morpurgo, J.E. *Master of None: An Autobiography.* Manchester: Carcanet, 1990.

Penton, Brian. *The Art of William Dobell.* Present Day Art in Australia Series. Sydney: Ure Smith, 1946.

Peters Corbett, David. *The Modernity of English Art, 1914-30.* Manchester and New York: Manchester University Press, 1997.

Read, Benedict and Thistlewood, David, eds. *Herbert Read: A British Vision of World Art.* Leeds: Leeds City Art Galleries, in association with The Henry Moore Foundation and Lund Humphries, 1993.

Read, Herbert. ed. *Unit 1, The Modern Movement in English Architecture, Painting and Sculpture.* London: Cassell and Company, 1934.

Reichardt, Jasia. *Victor Pasmore.* London: Metheun, 1962.

Richardson, John. *The Sorcerer's Apprentice: Picasso, Provence, and Douglas Cooper.* London: Jonathan Cape, 1999.

Ross, Alan *Colours of War: War Art 1939-45.* Foreword by Kenneth Clark. London: Jonathan Cape, 1983

Rothenstein, Sir John. *British Art Since 1900: An Anthology.* London: Phaidon, 1962.

Rothenstein, Sir John. *Modern English Painters.* 3 vols. London: MacDonald and Co, 1984.

Spalding, Frances. *Duncan Grant.* London: Chatto and Windus, 1997.

Spalding, Frances. *Roger Fry, Art and Life.* London: Granada, 1980.

Secrest, Meryle. *Kenneth Clark, a Biography.* London: Weidenfeld and Nicolson, 1984.

Shone, Richard. *Bloomsbury Portraits, Vanessa Bell, Duncan Grant and their Circle.* London: Phaidon, 1993.

Smith, Matthew. *Matthew Smith.* Introduction by Sir Philip Hendy, Biographical Note by Francis Halliday and John Russell. London: George Allen and Unwin, 1962.

Steen, Marguerite. *William Nicholson*. London: Collins, 1943.
The Book Production War Economy Agreement, The Schedule with an Introduction and some Notes on Interpretation. London: The Publishers Association, 1942.
Unwin, Sir Stanley. *The Truth about a Publisher, an Autobiographical Record*. London: George Allen & Unwin, 1960.
West, Anthony. *John Piper*. London: Secker and Warburg, 1979.
Williams, Sir William Emrys. *The Penguin Story,* Penguin: Harmondsworth, 1956.
Williams, William Emrys. *Allen Lane, A Personal Portrait*. London: The Bodley Head, 1973.
Weybright, Victor. *The Making of a Publisher, A Life in the 20th Century Book Revolution*. London: Weidenfeld and Nicolson, 1968.
World War Two, A Display of Pictures from the Collection to Mark the 50th Anniversary of the Outbreak of War in September 1939. Introduction by Penelope Curtis. Liverpool: Tate Gallery, 1989.